Matthew Canfield Read

Archeology of Ohio

Matthew Canfield Read

Archeology of Ohio

ISBN/EAN: 9783744659338

Printed in Europe, USA, Canada, Australia, Japan

Cover: Foto ©Andreas Hilbeck / pixelio.de

More available books at **www.hansebooks.com**

ARCHÆOLOGY

OF OHIO.

By M. C. READ.

LATE OF THE GEOLOGICAL SURVEY OF OHIO; TRUSTEE
OF OHIO ARCHÆOLOGICAL SOCIETY IN CHARGE AT
PHILADELPHIA, 1876; AND ASSISTANT COM-
MISSIONER AT THE EXPOSITION AT
NEW ORLEANS IN 1884-5.

PUBLISHED BY
The Western Reserve Historical Society,
CLEVELAND, OHIO.

Approved for publication:
>LEE MCBRIDE,
>H. G. CLEVELAND,
>SAM BRIGGS,
>>*Committee on Printing.*

CLEVELAND LEADER PRINT.

TABLE OF CONTENTS.

	PAGE.
The Archaeological Exhibit,	7
Flint or Chert Implements.	8
Arrow Points,	10
Knives.	11
Scrapers, Drills and Perforators.	22
Chert Spades and Hoes,	22
Stone Implements,	25
Axes and Battle Axes.	25
Hammer Stones.	33
Celts, Skinners, Etc.,	34
Plumb Balls, Sinkers and Pendants.	35
Mortars and Pestles,	36
Cup Stones,	39
Discoidal Stones,	39
Stone Ornaments.	40
Bird-Shaped Ornaments,	42
Beads and Tubes.	42
Banner Stones, Badges, or Wands.	45
Pipes,	46
Hematite,	52
Bone and Horn Implements.	52
Copper Implements,	53
Pottery,	54
Shells,	56
Rock Shelters,	56
Human Effigies.	61
Fire Hearths,	64
Picture Writing and Inscribed Rocks.	65
Earthworks.	79
Mining by the Mound Builders,	100
Alphabetic Writing and Engraved Tablets.	101
Social and Civil Condition of the Mound Builders.	109
Were the Mound Builders the First Occupants?	113
Addendum—What is It?	118

INTRODUCTION.

During this centennial year of Ohio, the attention of its citizens will be generally directed to its past.

The State is remarkable for the number and extent of its earthworks, no spot of equal size on the globe having so many and so extensive monuments of earth.

Whether one stands on the grounds of the Agricultural Society, in Licking County, inside the thirty-acre circle, with its high walls shutting out all view of modern civilization, and remembers that this was only one of many works extending for miles in more than one direction; whether, as happened to me last summer, he spends three and a half hours clambering along the steep embankments of Fort Ancient, or whether he reads in books alone of these and various wonderful works, remembering again that there are over ten thousand mounds in the State, he will be alike amazed at such and so many remains left by a race so far unknown that it can as yet simply be styled "The Mound Builders."

The interest has been romantic, and the temptation, in absence of evidence, to exercise the imagination, has been quite irresistible. As years have flown and knowledge from many investigators has been added up, it is time that archaeology shall begin to be certain and a science. The next step requires a competent experience and a sound judgement to decide both what is and what is not proven. For to be right it is quite important to know the limits and certainties of knowledge.

This Society presents to its members with pleasure this little book, by Professor M. C. Read, of Hudson, Ohio, late a prominent member of the Geological Survey, of the State. He was also, in 1876, the most active Trustee of the State Archaeological Society of Ohio, in charge, with the late

President of our Society, Colonel Charles Whittlesey, of the Archaeological Exhibit of the State at the Philadelphia Exhibit. Later he was in 1884–5 Assistant Commissioner at the Exposition at New Orleans, having in charge the archaeological exhibit there.

His tastes, experiences, and mental habits, have been such that we think ourselves fortunate in making this, in this centennial year, the first of our new series of publications.

It has been desired that at this time this publication should be made, and hoped that it will be of value in assisting knowledge and directing attention to this subject which it is to be hoped is this year to have the advantage of the largest exhibitions within the State itself.

This book was mainly prepared for a report upon this subject and most of the illustrations were prepared for it as such and in outline as the amount to be devoted to engraving was small. The author acknowledges his indebtedness to this Society, to the Smithsonian Institution, to Mr. Robert Clarke, of Cincinnati, and Mr. Peter Neff, of Gambier, for the use of engravings and for copies of others. Some of them have appeared in former tracts of the Society, but it has been thought best that Professor Read should be able to present, though not a complete, a typical treatise upon his subject.

C. C. BALDWIN,
President of the Western Reserve Historical Society,
of Cleveland, Ohio.

The Archæological Exhibit.

By M. C. READ, Assistant Commissioner,
Hudson, Ohio.

The general attention now given to archaeological studies makes all good exhibits of local archaeology important features in general exhibitions. This was made apparent at the Centennial Exhibition in Philadelphia. No part of that great exhibit of the industries and arts of the world attracted greater attention of all classes, than the pre-historic relics of the nations represented. The beginnings of civilization, the rude attempts of primitive man everywhere, to conquer the forces of nature, and provide for his ever-increasing wants, are now more carefully studied than ever before. And as there is no State in the Union richer in archaeological remains than Ohio, it was eminently fitting that the exhibit made at New Orleans, intended to illustrate the arts, industries, resources and civilization of this State, should be accompanied by a like exhibit of its pre-Columbian inhabitants.

The brief time which could be given to making the collections for this exhibit, rendered the making of such a collection as was desirable, wholly impossible. If all of the collections great and small in the State could be examined, and permission obtained to use selected specimens, which were well authenticated, accompanied with descriptions showing when, where and under what conditions they were found, an exhibit could be made which would enable us to commence an accurate classification of these remains, and to understand at least approximately their significance. Before these typical and valuable specimens are lost or carried out of the State, such a collection ought to be made, either by the State, or by some society, so organized, as to insure the preservation of the collection, in some central locality, where it would be accessible to all students of archaeology. Every year's delay renders the making of such a collection more difficulty, and would make the collection of less value when made. Its preservation could be fully insured by making it the property of the State, to be treated as a part of the library of the history of the State.

In making the selections for the New Orleans Exhibition, many collections could not be visited. Many owners were unwilling, for any monied guarantee, to risk the loss of specimens, and reliance had to be made upon the generosity and public spirit of those who were willing to entrust their whole collections to the care of the Commission. Messrs. Baldwin and Bauder, of the Northern Ohio and Western Reserve Historical Society, of Cleveland; The Ohio State University, of Columbus; Thomas W. Kinney, of Portsmouth; R. W. Mercer and S. C. Heighway, of Cincinnati, are entitled to the special thanks of the Committee for their generosity in this particular.

FLINT OR CHERT IMPLEMENTS.

Of the many thousand articles exhibited, the so-called "flint" implements were the most numerous, and these, from the great variety of forms, and often from their delicacy and perfect workmanship, attract the most attention. They are not made of a true flint, but of a flint-like chert, found in place on the horizons of the carboniferous limestones of the State. Many ancient quarries have been noticed from which this material was mined, the most extensive one being on Flint Ridge, southeast of Newark, in Licking county. Here many acres are covered, to a depth of several feet, with the broken fragments of chert, taken from the quarries.

The miners had learned that the chert exposed to atmospheric agencies did not chip readily, and was poorly adapted to their work. Accordingly they rarely attacked the stratum at its outcrop, but sunk pits to it, where it was covered with several feet of earth. These they carried through the chert, undermined it, and could thus easily work out the blocks into which it was naturally divided. The value they attached to this material is indicated by the vast amount of waste now remaing upon the surface. Not more than one or two per cent., of the material quarried, would be available for the production of the bettter class of flint implements. The selected material was apparently largely carried to other places to be manufactured, and was probably an article of barter between separated communities. Many places have been noted, remote from these ancient quarries, where the surface soil is filled with chips and flakes, and where broken arrows, knives and spears are conspicuously abundant.

The typical fossils of the limestones are sparingly found in the chert, and are occasionally seen in the finished implements — reliable witnesses of the material. Two such specimens from my small collection were on exhibition.

In Mr. Kinney's collection was a large number of beautiful specimens, called by the Archaeologists of the Smithsonian Institute, "leaf-shaped implements." These were a part of a single find of nearly four hundred specimens, and a large number of such finds have been made in the State. Rarely seen scattered upon the surface, they are found deposited by hundreds beneath the surface, and, in every case, where definite information can be obtained, on the margin of a stream or lake where they would be kept constantly moist. None of them are notched or fitted to be attached to handles. They appear to be unfinished implements, chipped into form and burried where the flaking character of the material would not be impaired, and to be afterward fitted for their special uses.

It is related that when the Angel met Moses at the Inn and sought to kill him, his wife, Zippora, evidently supposing that his danger arose from the fact that he had neglected to subject their son to the Abrahamic rite, seized a "sharp stone," and with it circumcised their child, when the Angel departed. The word rendered "sharp stone" in the Septuagint version means a pebble from the brook, indicating that the author of the narrative understood that a stone, from which a knife could be extemporized, must be taken from the water. It is also related that the California Indians, in want of a knife, will search in the nearest stream for a stone, chip it to an edge, and with it skin a deer almost as quickly as he could with a modern steel knife. The primitive inhabitants of Ohio were doubtless equally well informed, and would preserve their unfinished implements where their flaking qualities would not be impaired. One of these deposits, in Summit County, contained also a number of pieces of matamorphic slate, chipped into the form of the polished stone ornaments, common in the State, but neither perforated or polished.

ARROW POINTS.

What are "arrow points?" is a question which would be differently answered by different collectors. A correct answer to this question, and many others which will arise in an attempted classification, can perhaps be reached by learning—

First. How tribes, still making flint implements, use them.

Second. What is the form of the first substitutes for them made of metal?

Third. What light does any well-authenticated picture writing shed upon the question?

Now all the flint arrow tips, anywhere obtained, attached to shafts, are very small in comparison with many so-called arrows in most collections, and the modern Indian, who still uses the bow, and has adopted iron or steel for his arrow tips, makes them all small. It is obvious also that the large pieces could be used for arrow points only at short range, and with very strong bows.

In the illustrations, figure No. 8 represents a very delicate glass arrow point made by a Tin Tin California Indian; Nos. 19 and 20, chert points, attached to shafts in the Smithsonian collection, made by McCloud River Indians; Nos. 21 and 22, similar points in the same collection, made by Hoopah Indians, and Nos. 24, 25 and 26, iron points, attached to shafts in the Montana exhibit.

With these may be compared Nos. 1 to 18, inclusive, representing the different forms and sizes of what may properly be called Ohio arrow points. But there is a gradual increase in size, and no definite line can be drawn between the arrow points and the larger forms.

KNIVES.

Chert and rock fragments, which could be chipped to a sharp edge, constituted the only material largely available for the manufacture of cutting implements for primitive men, and natural wants would prompt to the extensive use of this material for such purposes. The forms of the implements, the specimens still found in use attached to their short handles, and the few specimens found, in which the handle is wrought out of the same material as the knife, and constituting a part of it, clearly indicate the character of these implements.

The rudest form is made without any attempt at symmetry, without any provision for the attachment of a handle, and is simply a rock fragment chipped to a single cutting edge. A collection of such knives, taken from a rock shelter in Boston, Summit County, was among the exhibits. Nearly all found at that place were of this character—fragments of shale, quartz, boulders, and other rock, so broken as to give a single cutting edge, of such forms as Nos. 27 and 28 in the

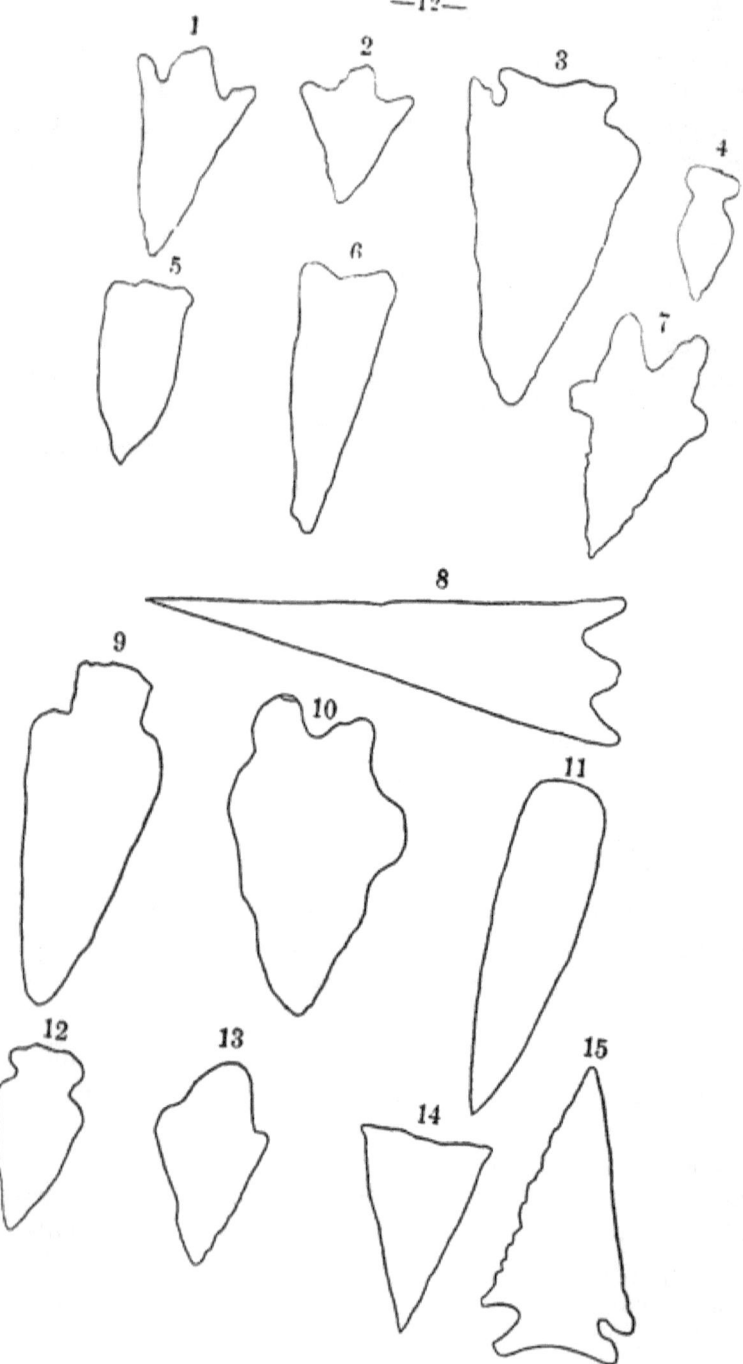

—13—

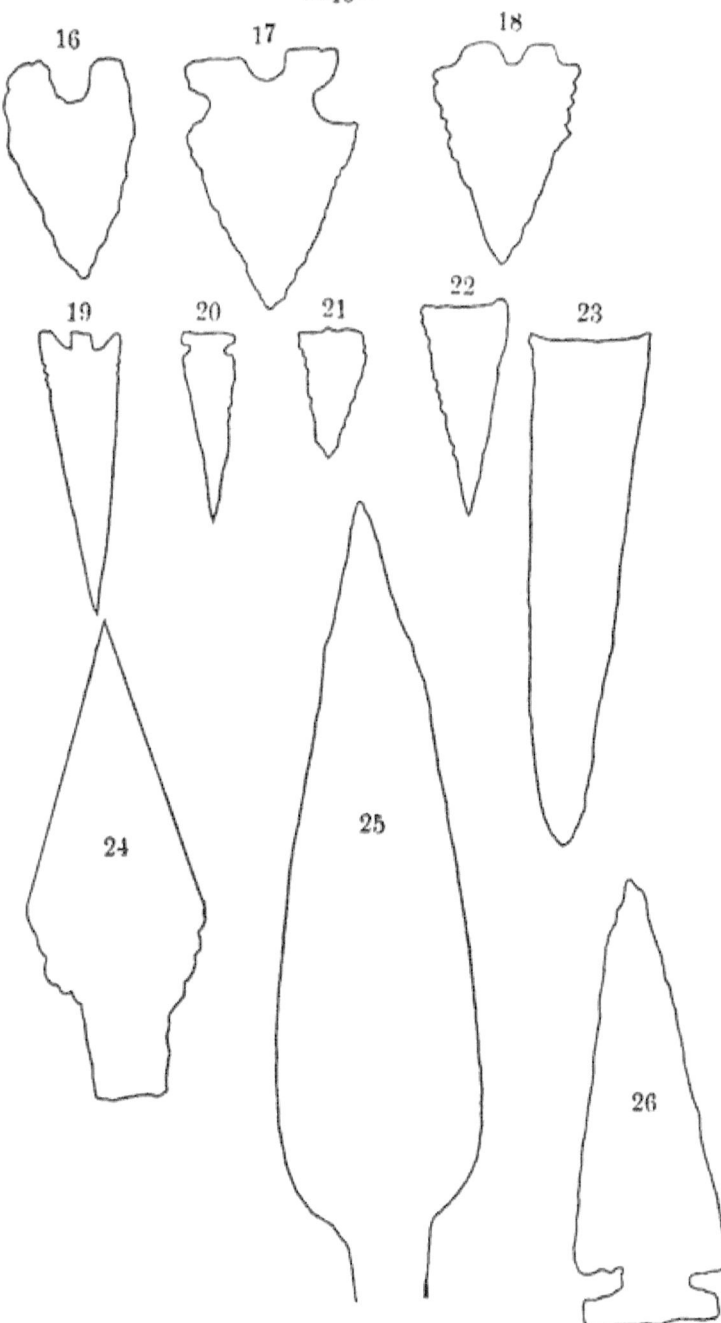

illustrations. From the ash-bed of this shelter seventy-five such knives were gathered, made from all the material available for such uses, to be found in the neighborhood, and the uses for which they were intended could not be mistaken.

Figure 29 represents one of several specimens of handled flint knives in the Smithsonian collection, reduced one-half diameter.

No. 3930, of the Smithsonian collection, is a knife of red jaspery chert, obtained from a mound on Warrior River, Alabama, of which the handle is of the same material as the knife, the whole being of one piece. This is also in figure No. 30, reduced one-half.

Figure No. 31 represents a similar knife from the same collection, and No. 32, still a different form, made of white chert, in the Missouri collection, both reduced one-half.

These illustrations sufficiently show the manner of attaching handles to these implements, which were doubtless used, so far as their wants required, for all the purposes for which modern cutting implements are used. When all the collections in the State are collated and compared, it is probable that specimens from the mounds may be distinguished from later forms, and that a discrimination can be made between local tribal forms. Marked distinctions can now be seen between collections made in different places, in part due to the differences in the character of the material used, and doubtless in part due to the skill and taste of the manufacturers.

The forms are almost endless, and pass by incessable gradations into the forms which in collections are classified as daggers and spears. Illustrations of a few of the most typical forms will be given.

Figure 33 represents a very beautiful specimen, found deeply buried in the glacial drift in Twinsburgh, Summit County.

—15—

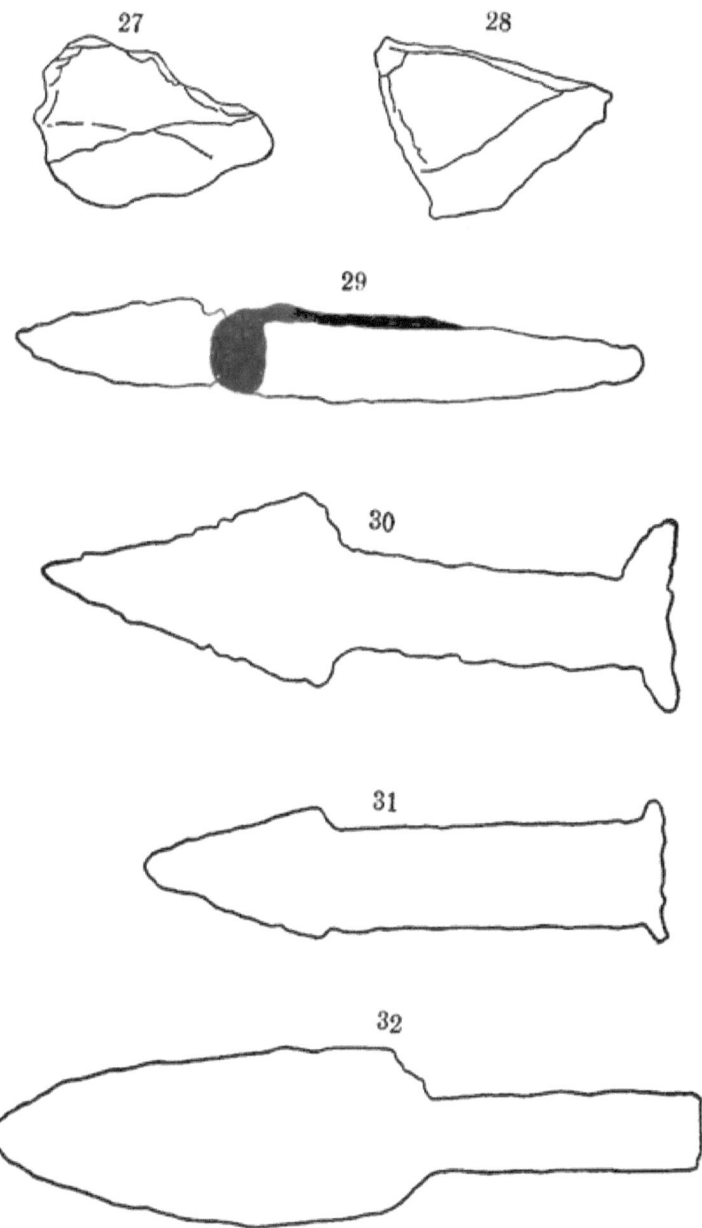

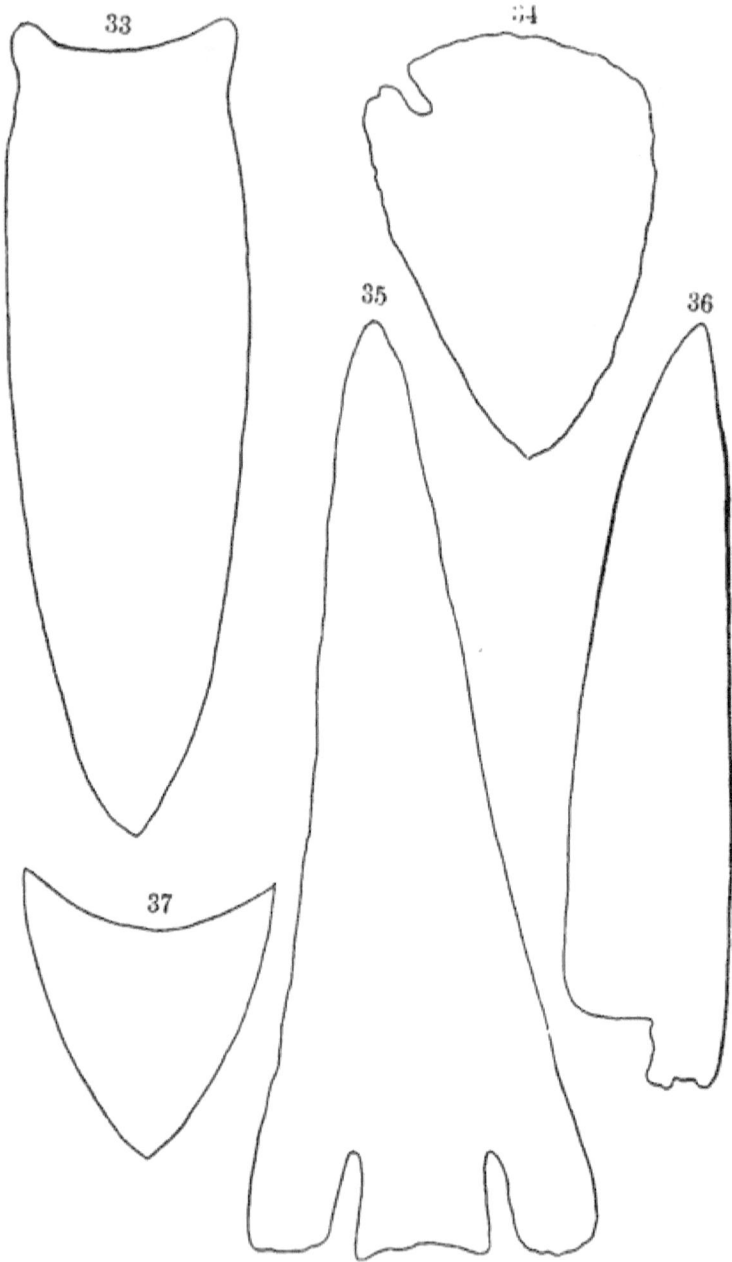

It has a highly polished, reddish surface, supposed to indicate great antiquity. A precisely similar specimen was in the Rhode Island Exhibit at the Centennial. Mr. Thomas Cleany has, in his very valuable collection at Cincinnati, two such specimens taken from a mound in Missouri; and Mr. Thomas W. Kinney has also one which was on exhibition in his collection at New Orleans, but the locality from which it was obtained is not given.

A similar form, of yellow jasper, from California, is figured in the description of the typical specimens in the Smithsonian Collection.

This peculiar form, from widely separated localities—all the specimens, so far as appears, are very old—some of them from mounds, tends to the conclusion that the Indians occupying, at least the northern part of the United States upon its discovery by Europeans, were preceded by a more artistic people.

Attempting to make no distinction between knives, daggers, and spear points, illustrations of some of the most marked forms are given in the plates of illustrations, figures No. 33 to 66 inclusive. Some of these, particularly No. 36, from Indiana, and No. 46, from North Carolina, are remarkably similar to modern knife-blades. Quite a large number of the arrow-point form, are symmetrically beveled on the opposite sides of the two edges, of which No. 40, from Knox county, is an illustration. This specimen carries a characteristic fossil of the coal measure limestone.

This form is by many regarded as intended to give a rotary motion to the missile, but this is very doubtful. Most of these beveled specimens are too large for arrow-points, and if used for spear-points, the small surface of the beveled edges would not give the rotary motion to a heavy missile. This form may be the result of the peculiar character of the material, the symmetrical beveling being determined by the position in which the object was held when chipped. Or, if designed, the object may have been to get a stronger cutting or scraping edge than would result from a flatter chipping.

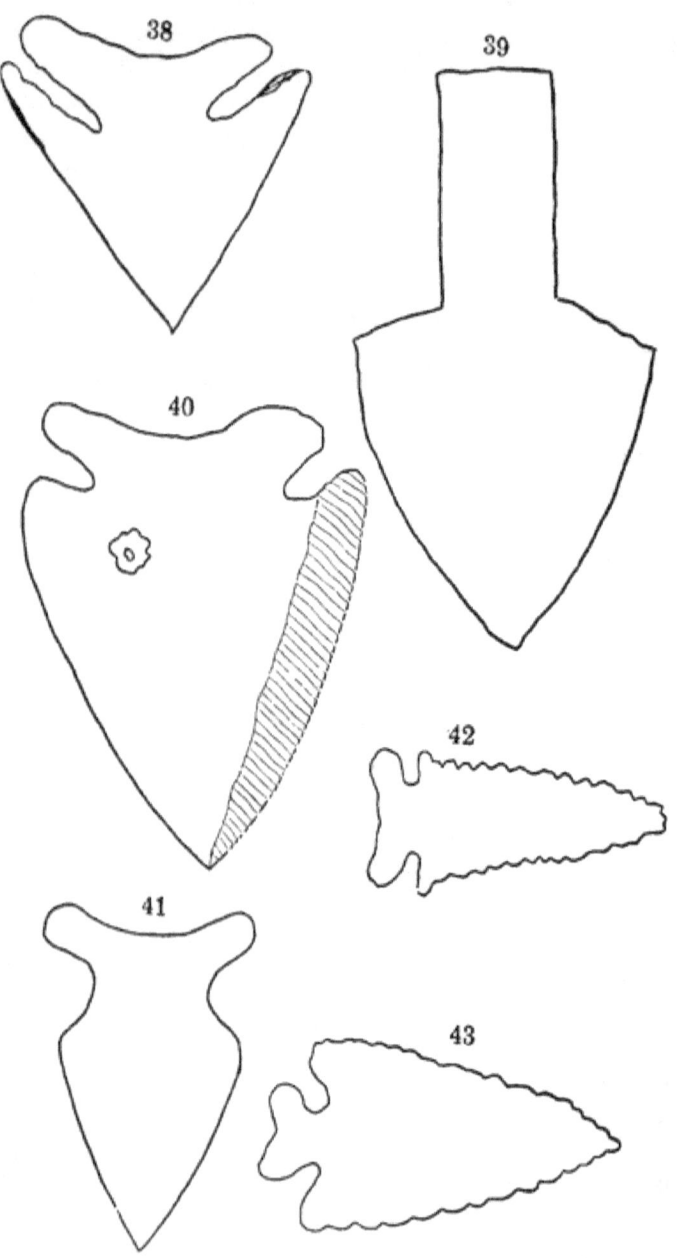

Figures 39, from Mr. Kinney's collection, and 47, from Knox County, illustrate forms abundant in the southern part of the State. They are all very thick, short and broad, with long and strong shanks by which they were apparently fastened into sockets; none of them have notches to aid in binding them in place. Figure 87 illustrates, probably, one of the uses of this form. It is a modern war-club with an iron tooth, doubtless of the form of the flint tooth formerly used. Bancroft, in his "Native Races of the Pacific States," Vol. IV., page 210, gives an illustration of Yucatan sculpture, in which a figure is represented armed with probably what the Spanish invaders called stone swords, consisting of a club into which was fastened four chipped stones or flints; the weapon is illustrated in figure 88. These stout Ohio forms were very probably used in a similar manner.

Figure 45, from S. C. Heighway's collection, represents a form found in nearly all the collections in the southwest part of the State. All are very symmetrical, very elegantly chipped, generally of pretty large size, the specimen figured being one of the smallest. The shank is often very much smaller than that of the one figured, and often so delicate that if fastened to a handle it would be very liable to be broken. Every modern man or boy is not equipped for work or play, without his pocket knife; and it is suggested that the notched shanks of these and similar forms were not made, at least in all cases, for the purpose of attaching handles, but rather for attaching strings, by which the knives were securely tied to the clothing, to be always ready for all the uses made of the modern pocket knife.

Figure 53, from Logan County, is beautifully toothed on each edge, and is a remarkably delicate specimen of chipping. It could not be designed for use as an ordinary knife or spear, but was probably used as a kind of saw.

No. 44 is of white chert, very beautifully chipped, and was picked up on the site of an old manufactory of chert

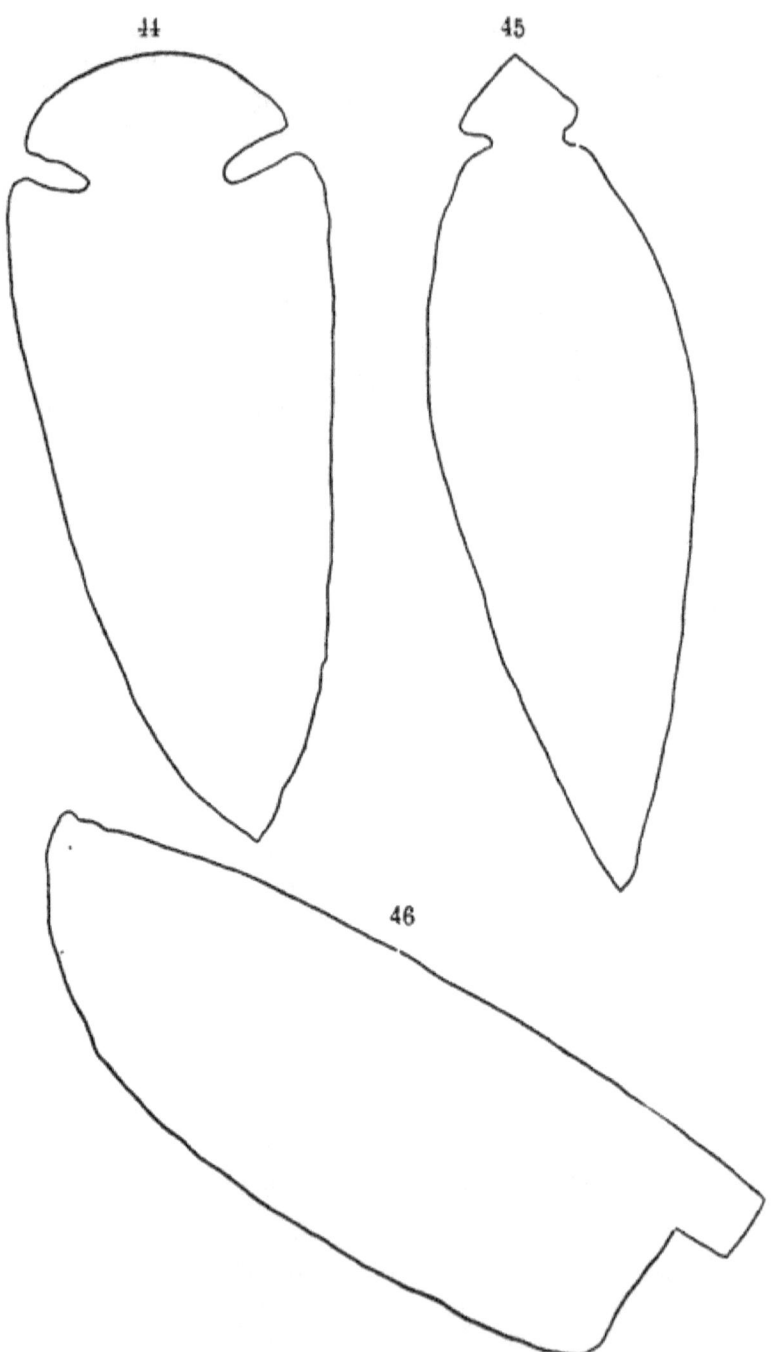

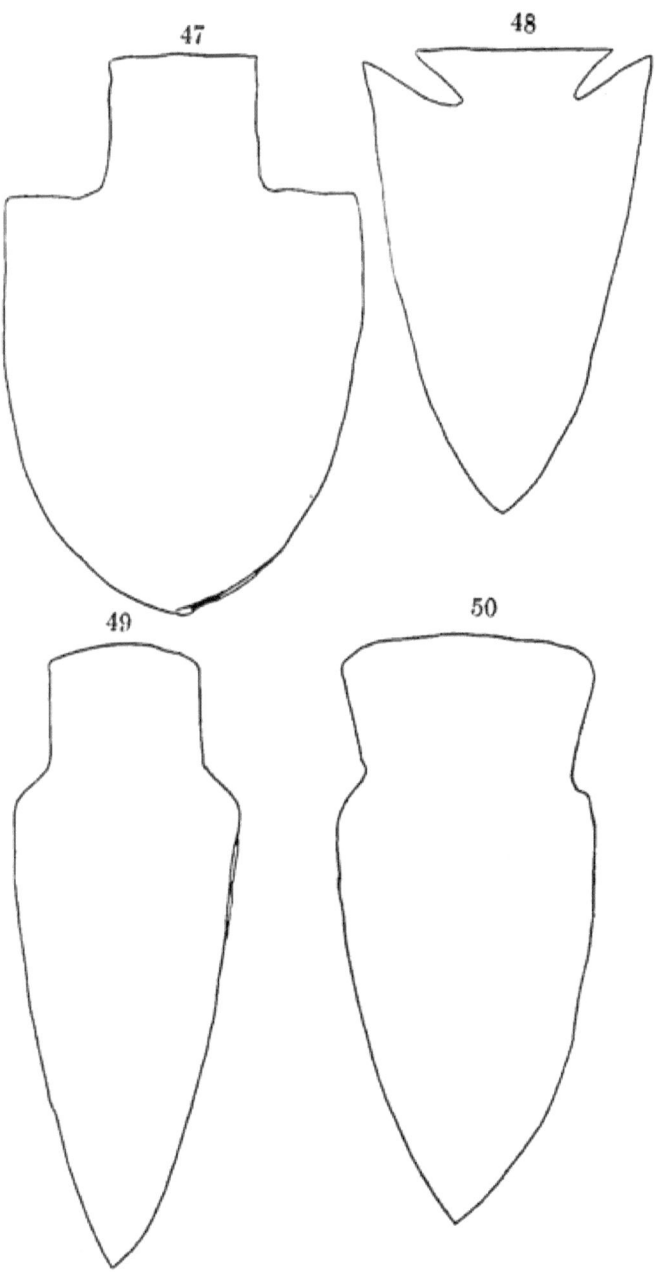

implements in the northern part of Trumbull County, and at a remote distance from any natural deposit of chert.

SCRAPERS, DRILLS AND PERFORATORS.

Figures 67 to 79 illustrate some of the forms of drills and scrapers from Mr. Kinney's collection, and 80, 81, and 84, specimens from Mr. Heighway's collection. There is almost an endless variety of forms, and some of them show wonderful skill in the art of chipping.

Figures 82, 83, and 85, represent specimens put on exhibition at Philadelphia by H. H. Hill, of Cincinnati, and are introduced to show some of the most unusual forms.

Figure 86 is quite unique, and illustrates a specimen belonging to Florien Giouque, Esq., of Cincinnati. The peculiar form is plainly designed, and not the result of accident, or of any flaw in the material. He calls it a fish spear, and the name may stand in default of a better one.

CHERT SPADES AND HOES.

Some remarkably excellent agricultural implements were put on exhibition, especially in the collection contributed by Mr. L. F. Bauder and Judge C. C. Baldwin, of Cleveland. Some of these were fully one foot long and six inches wide, chipped from chert in a way which would puzzle any modern artificer, with all his appliances, to imitate. Ordinary chert arrows and knives can be readily imitated, as the material yields to simple pressure upon the edges and can be flaked in shape. But how sufficient pressure could be applied to these large pieces to flake them into shape, and not entirely crush them, is a difficult problem to solve. These spades and hoes were attached to handles, and fastened in place by some material which covered from one-third to one-half their surfaces. This is shown by the limitation of the polished surface, as some of them have been used until the part brought into contact with the earth became as smooth as glass. Taking into account the difficulty in finding blocks of chert without

—23—

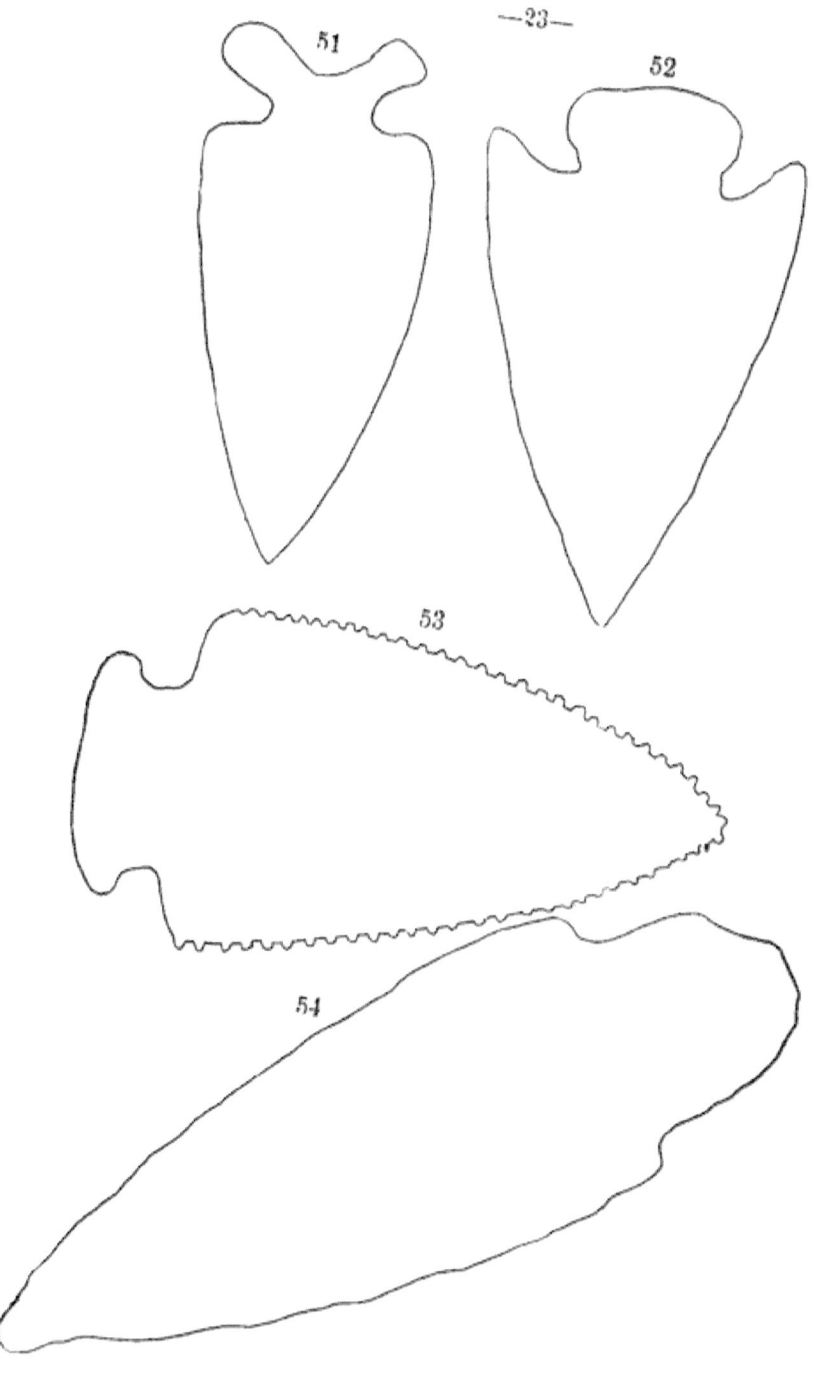

—24—

55

56

flaws, large enough for the production of these tools, and the labor required to shape them, it is probable that spades and hoes to-day, of beaten gold, would not cost as much in days' labor as these old implements cost. Surely in the sweat of their faces did these old agriculturists eat their bread.

STONE IMPLEMENTS.

The boulders of the drift furnished the great supply of material for what are ordinarily called stone implements. These are found in the State in great profusion and of a variety of forms, some very roughly wrought, and others very highly polished. But in Ohio material does not exist for the determination of a paleolithic and neolithic age, unless we limit the latter to post-Columbian times. Very delicately cut and highly polished pipes of catlinite are occasionally found, probably wrought with modern tools obtained from the whites. Several such specimens were obtained from small mounds near Monroeville, Huron County. In other places pipes of this material are found inlaid with lead ornaments. Of course these are quite modern. The carefully wrought pipes, and other articles obtained from the mounds, indicate greater skill in the working of stone than was manifested by the hunting tribes, who occupied the territory upon the advent of the white settlers. So that if we should seek for a rough stone age and a polished stone age, the latter would be prior in time. The builders of the mounds evidently had a higher social organization than the hunting tribes, and would naturally excel them in the rudiments of the arts of civilization.

AXES AND BATTLE-AXES.

The grooved axes are among the most remarkable of Ohio finds. They present a great variety of forms, and range in size from a weight of one to sixteen pounds. Some even of the largest are highly polished, very symmetrial in form, are

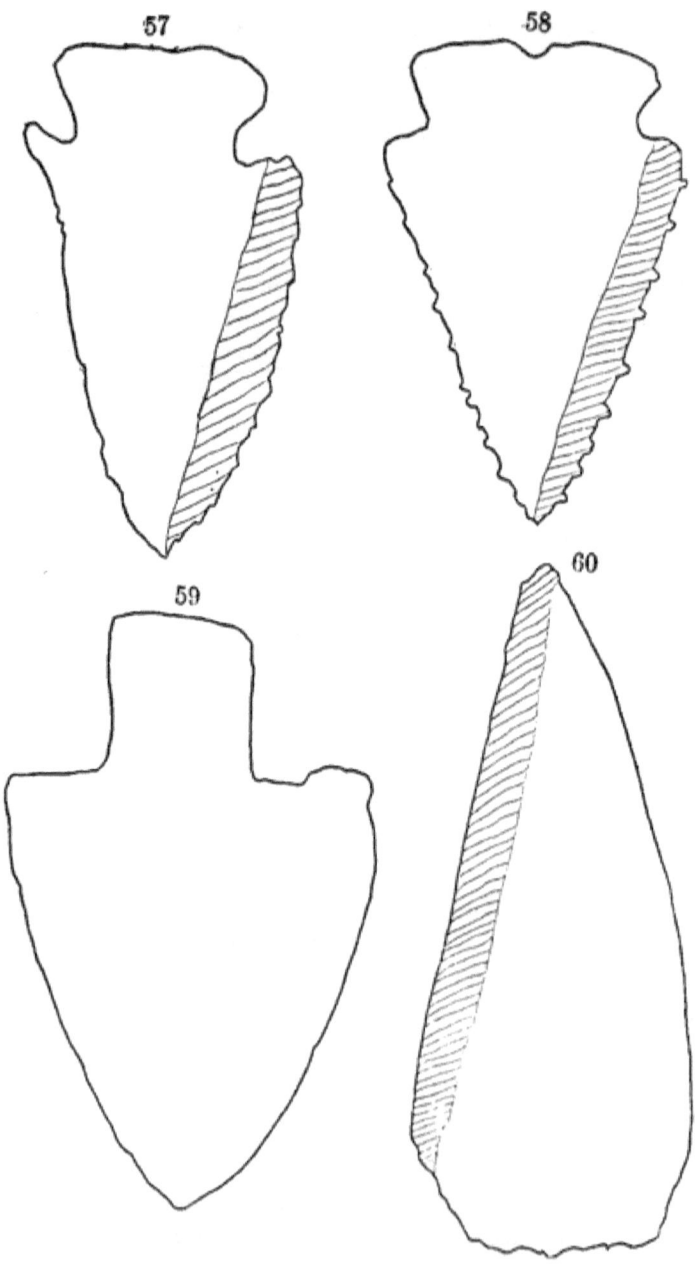

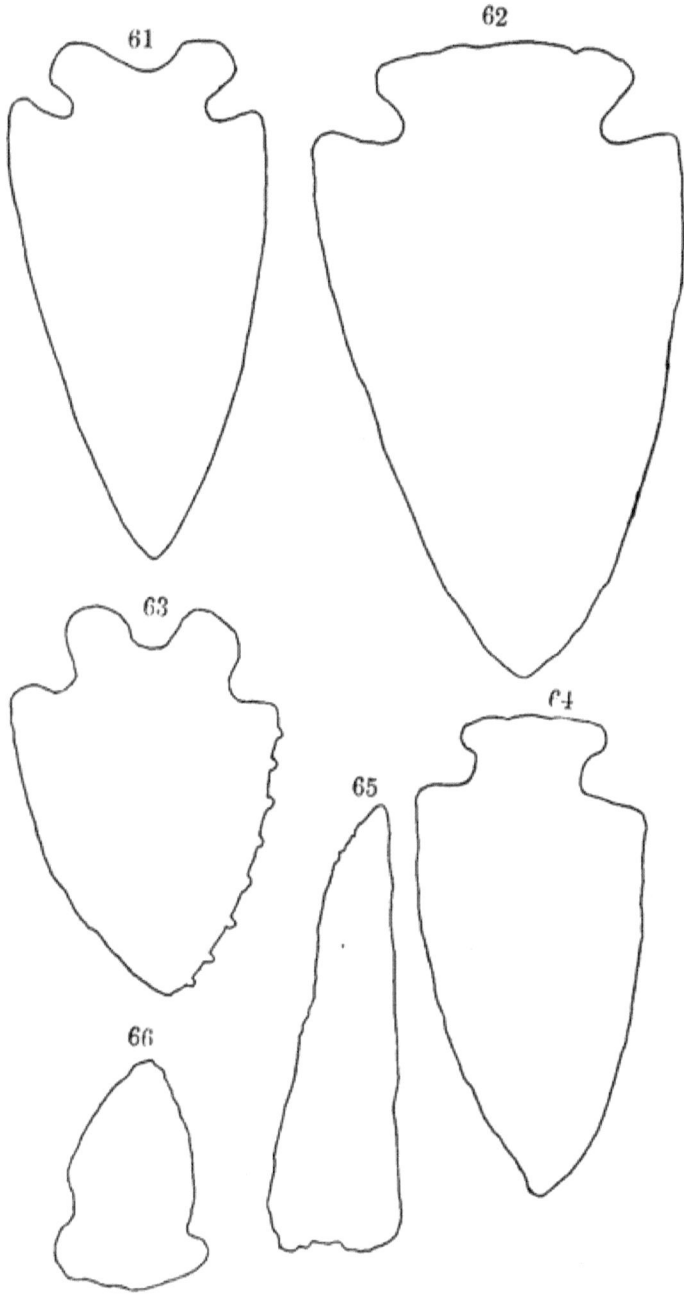

brought to as sharp an edge as the material will permit, each evidently representing many months of continuous labor.

Many of the forms indicate that they were handled by bending a flexible branch of the size of a small hoop-pole around the groove, and fastening it in place by thongs, or some similar material. A groove is sometimes made on one of the narrow sides, at right angles with the groove for the handle, and evidently intended to keep in place a wedge driven in to tighten the fastenings of the handle.

When we imagine one of the largest of these axes, with a handle proportioned, like the handle of a modern axe, we have to imagine with it a man to wield it, larger and stronger than Goliath, of Gath.

Through the kindness of W. H. Abbott, I obtained at the Exposition the cast of an axe found in Lake County, Illinois, at a place where several small mounds were plowed over. The axe and handle are wrought out of one piece, and the specimen doubtless illustrates the relative proportions of the axes and handles, when wooden handles were used, a proportion which must have been substantially preserved to enable any one to wield these large axes. The length of the axe, from poll to edge of bit, was seven inches; width of edge, four and a half inches; entire length of axe and handle, nine and three-fourths inches. It was intended to be used with one hand, and grasped so near to the axe the implement does not seem unwieldy. A greatly reduced outline of this axe is given in figure 93. Whether used in peaceful avocations, or as battle-axes, especially by foot soldiers, such short handles would be indispensable. For purposes of comparison, figures 95 are given, showing the size of battle axes in the hands of warriors, from sculptures copied by Rawlinson in his "Ancient Monarchies." At the right of each is a line showing the height of the figure of the soldier carrying the axe. Figure 94 is a copy of the battle-axe in the hands of a warrior, taken from one of the published cuts of the

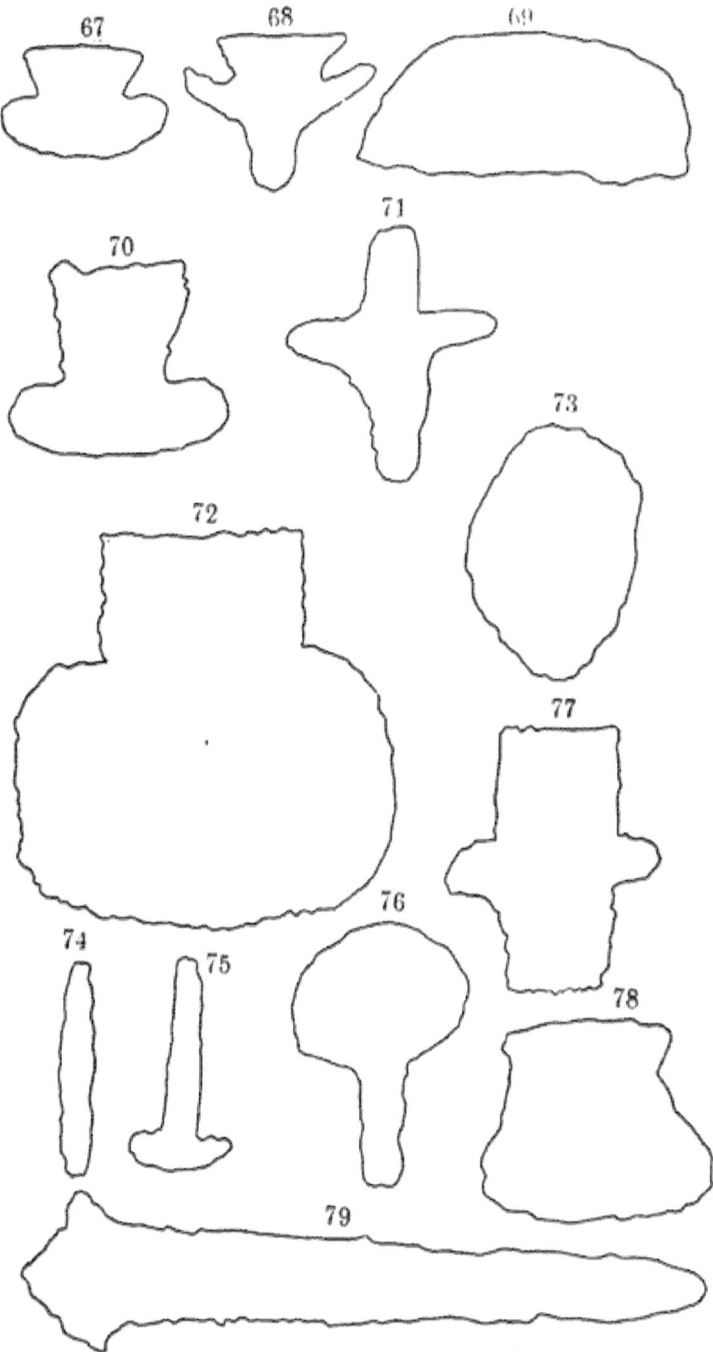

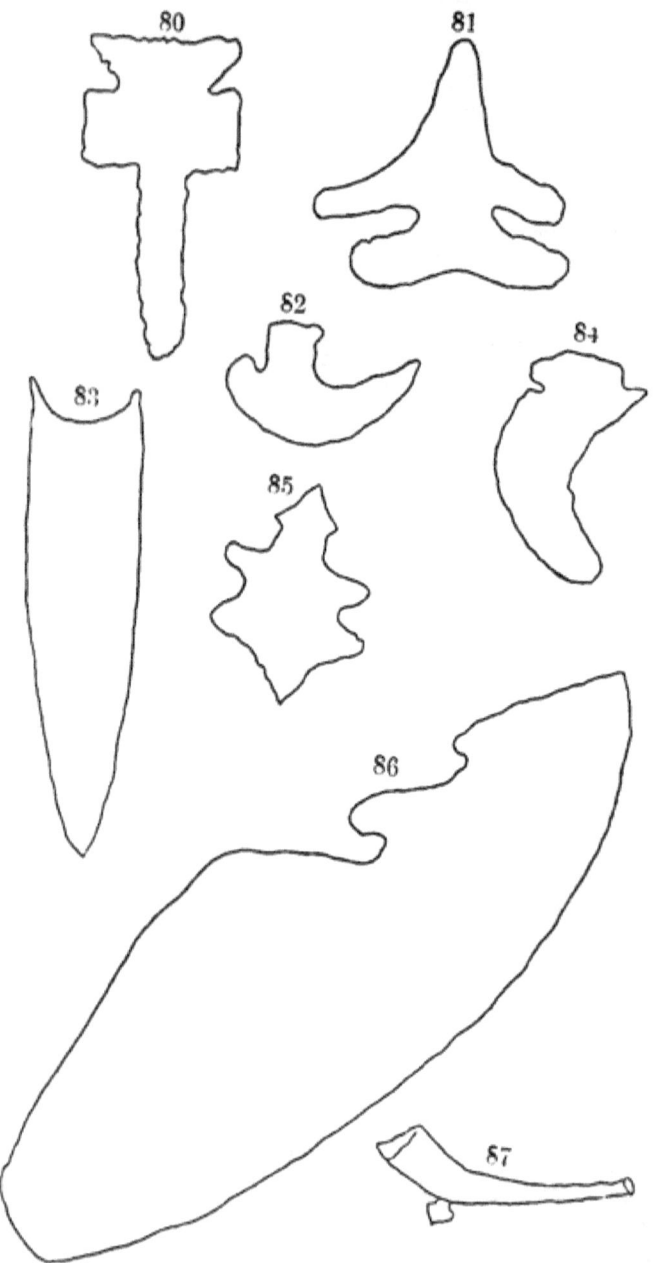

"Wilmington Inscribed Stones." The line at the right also shows the height in the engraving of the warrior carrying it. As he is evidently represented as on the war-path, carrying a spear in his left hand, and this battle-axe in the other, it is evident that the artist intended to represent an axe to be wielded with one hand. If the manner in which the axe is fastened to the handle is compared with the obvious mode of fastening two pieces, crossing each other at right angles as represented in figure 96, from a figure of a sculpture from Guatemala, and the use that is made of one of these delicate crescents of metamorphic slate, so common in Ohio, is noted, it will be evident that the artist committed about as many blunders as could be crowded into the delineation of a single object. If the relative proportions are observed, and the warrior was of the stature of six feet, the axe would be one foot long and with a handle of the length of about four and a half feet. It is attached to the handle in an impossible manner. An expensive ornament is attached to the end of the handle, the most inconvenient termination that could be devised, but which would fortunately be shattered by the first blow with the axe. Whoever may be the artist, and in whatever age he lived, he has certainly given us a fancy sketch of no value except to illustrate the skill and imagination of the artist.

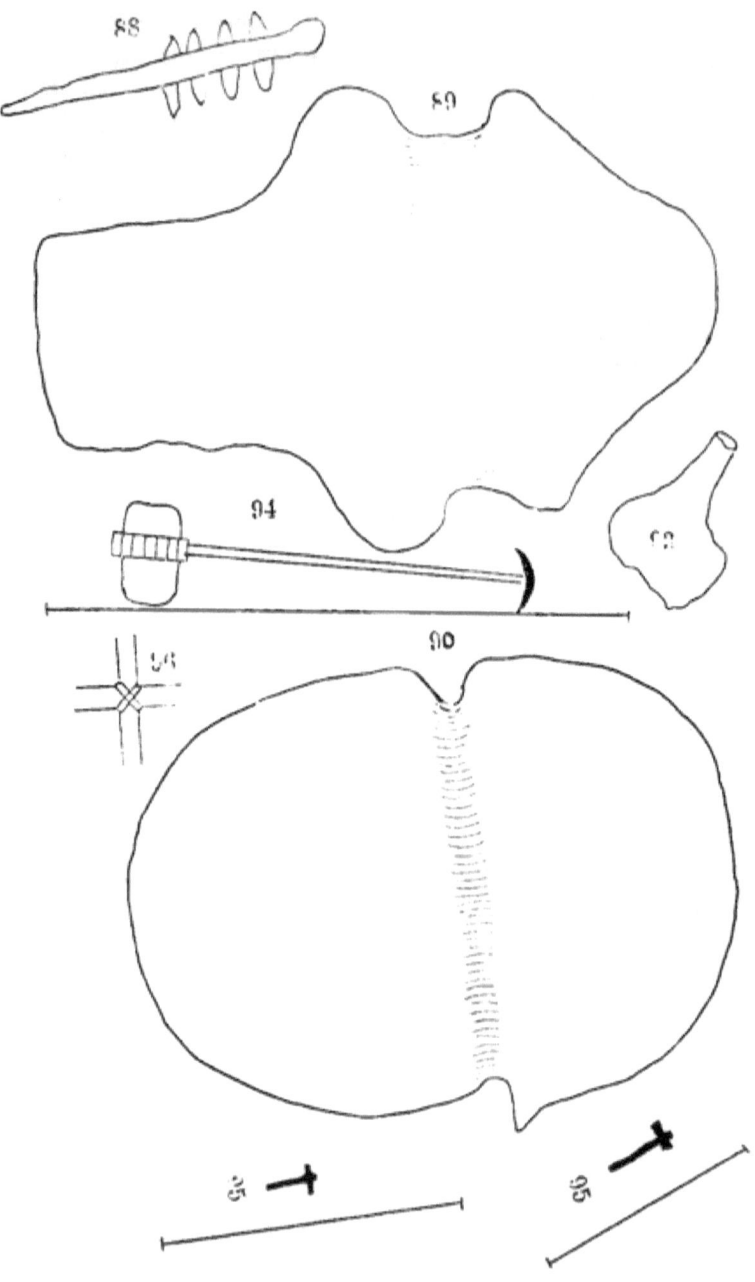

92

Figure 90 is a full-sized illustration of a very beautiful and highly polished ornamental axe, of bluish green metamorphic slate, found near Fort Hamilton, in Hamilton County, which, so far as known, is a unique specimen. Figures 89 and 92 represent more common forms reduced one-half.

A systematic classification of the different forms is impossible. The workmen apparently selected natural boulders as near the form and size of the utensil to be formed as possible, and worked them into a useful shape with as little labor as possible, so that the forms they finally assumed were often more the result of accident than of the design of the workman.

Not all of the axes are grooved; occasionally a double-grooved specimen is found, and one double-bitted axe was on exhibition. It will be apparent that none of these axes were efficient cutting implements, yet a specimen of wood taken from a mound, and belonging to the Ohio State University, shows that a log could be cut off with a nearly square butt with these stone axes, and the marks of the axe upon it indicate a rapidity of execution quite remarkable.

HAMMER STONES.

These are symmetrical stones, oblong or round—sometimes plain, sometimes grooved—and occasionally double-grooved, two grooves passing around the stone at right angles to each other. While commonly called hammer stones, specimens obtained from the Western Indians are conclusive evidence that they were sometimes used, with handles attached, as war clubs, and very likely were mainly designed for this use.

Sitting Bull's war club, exhibited in the Montana collection, is a symmetrical stone in the form of two cones, applied base to base, grooved at the centre, to which is attached a flexible handle covered with raw buffalo hide, by which it is attached to the stone. The handle is thirty inches long and the whole constitutes a very formidable weapon for hand to hand combat, in the hands of a mounted man. Specimens similar to this, with a stiff handle made of the leg bone of a deer, and ten or twelve inches long, all covered with rawhide, are used by unmounted Indians.

Another specimen in the Montana collection shows another similar mode of using these stone balls. A spherical stone, about two and a half inches in diameter, is neatly covered with rawhide, which at one side is continued into strings, braided into a stout cord a few inches long. The end of this cord is attached to a flexible handle, the whole forming a slung-shot with which an enemy could be terribly punished.

Grooved Hammer.
Rockport, Cuyahoga county, Ohio, ½ nature.

Figures on Trojans column represent the Kelts in battle, loaded with such stones, which they are using as missiles, some throwing them with the hand, others with a sling. They were doubtless used by our Indians for a variety of purposes, peaceful and warlike, and some of them by their abrasion show their continued use as hammer stones.

CELTS, SKINNERS, ETC.

Of these there was a very large variety in the exhibit. They are chisel-shaped stones of different sizes, all brought to an edge, and some showing long-continued use. By some they are called bark-peelers, and if their name was to be determined by the purpose for which they were most used, it is probable that this name would be adopted.

Lumbering, with the Indian, was bark-peeling, and there was nothing within his reach supplying so many of his wants with so little labor, as bark. An Indian Paley would find in the fact that at certain seasons of the year the bark was so easily separated from the growing tree, his most marked evidence of a beneficent design, intended for the comfort of the race. With the whole sheets of bark he built his houses; with the inner layers he made baskets, clothing, thread, cord, ropes, etc., and doubtless used it many ways not suspected by us. In the gathering and preparing of this material these implements would be used, and also many of the sharp or serrated edged chert knives. Until we can compile a history of their arts, we can not determine all the uses of any of these implements.

PLUMB-BALLS, SINKERS AND PENDANTS.

The forms of these are almost as numerous as the specimens: some spherical, some cylindrical, some oval, some simple circular disks; and the kinds of material of which they are made almost equally diverse. They all have this in common, that they are relatively small, and are so perforated as to be easily suspended by a string, or have a small groove in which a string can be tied, for purposes of suspension. In the collection of the Smithsonian Institute obtained from Alaska, are stone sinkers, one of which is *six and a half* inches long, and over an inch in diameter at the largest point, attached as sinkers to the lines furnished with hooks for fishing. One would be slow to suspect the use of so heavy stone sinkers with so small fishing lines as those in this exhibit. Almost all tribes have learned the art of fishing with hook and line, and specimens of hooks found in Ohio, as well as in all parts of the country, indicate the practice everywhere here of the art which good old Isaac Walton has made classical.

With lines made of bark and the coarse fibers available, and unevenly and poorly twisted, requisite strength would

—36—

require large lines, and these would require correspondingly heavy sinkers. Doubtless these articles were sometimes used for other purposes, but none of them are too heavy sinkers for fishing, and it is probable that they were oftener used for this than for any other purposes.

MORTARS AND PESTLES.

Natural instinct everywhere prompts to the crushing, or grinding of grain to prepare it for food, and the first flouring mill is composed of two stones, one of which can be used with the hand in crushing the grain poured upon the other. This would soon be developed into the pestle and mortar, so easily made and so efficient that civilized man everywhere reverts to their use when better appliances fail.

When the Confederate forces were driven from Mission Ridge, flouring mills were found scattered along the whole length of the ridge. Each consisted of the stump of a tree hollowed out with the axe, and a round boulder picked up in the neighborhood. With these the soldiers prepared the grain for their corn-dodger rations. In the bed of a stream in a forest, in the north part of Ashland County, is a granite boulder of considerable size, in the top of which a cavity of a capacity of a peck or more has been laboriously picked. It would have been carried away long ago, to do service in an archaeological collection as a splendid specimen of an Indian mortar, had it not been disclosed that it was the work of a pioneer hunter who remained long enough in that locality to raise small crops of corn, and needed a mill in which to grind it. It still deserves to be rescued from its retreat and preserved as an illustration of pioneer history.

The indigenous races here seem never to have advanced beyond the pestle and mortar, although the hand-mill of two stones, one turning upon the other, seems to be readily suggested by them. Such a mill is a machine—the pioneer of all machinery—and these races apparently made no machines. Tools and implements of a great variety of forms, with which the working power is muscular force, they had the skill to make, but not the skill to subject any of the forces of nature to their control. The hand-mill substitutes the force of gravity for muscular force.

The most intelligent animals use tools—the Gibbon fights with a war club, the monkey cracks nuts with a stone, and the elephant drives away the flies which annoy him, with a brush. The savage makes tools, but no machines. His bow and arrow and his blow-tube are not in the highest sense machines, for his muscular energy drives the missile.

The beginning of real civilization is made in the construction of machines by which the strength of animals and the forces of nature become a substitute for human muscular work. When the hand-mill is discovered, the force of the running stream is soon harnessed to it, and out of this combination grows the modern flouring mill with all its improvements. This first step was not made by these primitive races, and they must be classed as savages. While they did not advance beyond the mortar and pestle, they expended much labor upon them, and with very creditable results. As the mortars are generally very heavy, only two were put on exhibition, but the pestles were very numerous and of a great variety of forms. While they had no flouring mills, they prepared their grain both by the grinding and the roller process. The pestles with one broad, rounded end, were used for grinding; the long specimens, largest in the middle and tapering slightly toward each end, were used in the roller process as they are now used with the metate by the New Mexican and Pueblo Indians.

An unusual form of pestle is represented by figure 93, reduced one-half. It has a broad grinding surface, with a handle just long enough to be clasped with one hand and a peculiarly ornamented top. It was found upon the surface in Summit County. An illustration of a common form from the Cleveland Historical Society's Collection is also given, (figure 93a.)

Fig. 93a.

CUP STONES.

These are sometimes called nut stones, and oftener foot-rests for spindles. They are very common in the State, and have been picked up in large numbers at the site of a series of old fire hearths in Summit County. A large collection shows that the cavities were commenced by an instrument like a pick, which left a conical, rough cavity, and were finally shaped by rotating some object in the cavity. When brought to the size of about one inch in diameter, they were apparently no longer used, as new cavities are commenced near their margins which enlarged to the same size would cut into them. They are made on natural fragments of rock, in this locality almost exclusively the debris of the carboniferous conglomerate, a coarse sand-stone with a sharp grit. With few exceptions throughout the State they are made in similar rock. A single fragment often bears several of these cavities and sometimes on opposite sides. If used as spindle rests, it is strange that so coarse a stone is selected which would make the friction much greater than if a harder rock were used.

Dr. Rau reports that some of the specimens in the Smithsonian collection still show traces of red paint in the cavities, and it is possible they were generally used to grind down pieces of hematite for paint. The specimens from this locality show no indication that they were formed by cracking nuts.

DISCOIDAL STONES.

These, of various sizes, are tolerably abundant in the State, and some remarkably fine and large specimens were exhibited in the collection. Those of smaller size, and perforated at the center, were probably used as spindle weights. The larger and unperforated ones, perhaps in some game. Dr. Rau quotes from Adair a detailed description of the game of chungke as played with such discs, and this explanation of their use is the most probable one. See also "Relics of the Mound Builders," Western Reserve Historical Society Tract No. 23, by C. C. Baldwin.

STONE ORNAMENTS.

The metamorphic slate, found in the drift, was the favorite material for the manufacture of stone ornaments. It is often beautifully banded, is moderately hard, takes a fine polish, and is not easily broken or scratched. Oblong pieces, generally called "shuttles," are very abundant. Of these there are a great many forms, generally with two perforations on a central line, each one generally about equi-distant from the center and one of the ends. These holes are apparently counter-sunk, so that if attached to the clothing by cords passing through the holes, having a knot at the end, the knot would be below the surface. Unfinished specimens show that in perforating them, conical drills were used, giving a counter-sunk form to the holes. It has been suggested that they were used as shuttles in weaving, in smoothing sinews or cords drawn through the holes, or in twisting double-stranded cords, but the holes are almost uniformly as perfect as when first drilled, and either of these uses would quickly destroy their symmetry—certainly the striae left by the drill. That they were not made purely for ornaments, is indicated by the fact that a much coarser material than this ornamental slate is sometimes used in making them. An unfinished specimen from fine grained yellow Waverly sand-stone was picked up in Summit County, and a rock-shelter in the same county, in which all the remains were exceedingly rude, yielded one specimen from Waverly shale, unpolished, unperforated, but which had apparently been abraded or worn longitudinally on one side by a softer material than that by which it was formed.

It may have been attached to the left arm as a protection against the bow-string, and it is possible that the more perfet specimens were used for the same purpose. This use is rendered more probable by the fact that specimens are found in graves in such position as indicates that they were attached to the arm of the buried body.

—41—

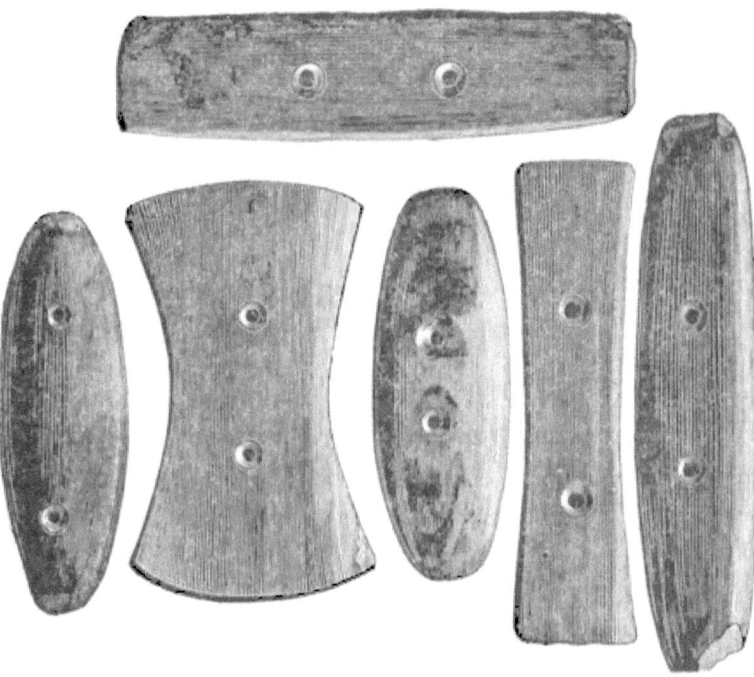

¼ Nature. Assorted Shuttles from Stones—Northern Ohio; Collection of the Fire Lands Historical Society.

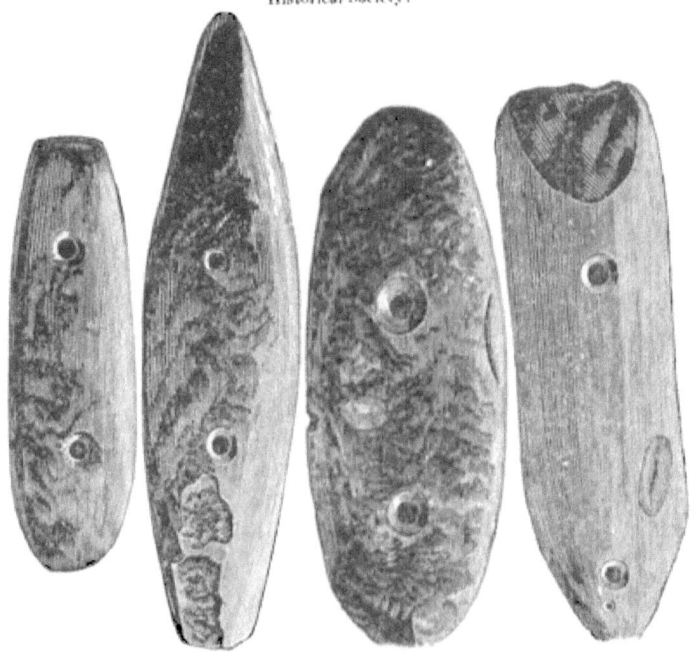

¼ Nature. Assorted Shuttles from Stones—Northern Ohio: Collection of the Fire Lands Historical Society.

BIRD-SHAPED ORNAMENTS.

These were largely represented in the collection, and are abundant in Ohio. They are formed out of this ornamental slate, and in most of the specimens the bird-form is very clearly intended. Some of them have projecting eyes that give them a strange appearance. They all have this peculiarity in common with several other ornamental forms into which this material is worked. On a central line at the base of each end a hole is drilled diagonally through the corner by which the ornament could be sewed to the clothing or other fabric in such a manner that the thread by which it was fastened in place would be concealed. Other ornamental pieces, of such form as not to admit of these concealed holes, are drilled through the central line from the top, the holes being so conical that a knot at the end of a cord drawn through the hole would be concealed, and the same result obtained, that is, the mode of fastening would be concealed.

In the collection of Dr. Griste, of Summit County, is one of these ornamental stones, exhibiting that peculiar polish which shows long continued use, while the striae left in drilling the diagonal holes are not worn down in the slightest degree.

BEADS AND TUBES.

Ornamental beads, sometimes nearly two inches in diameter, and flattened upon one side, composed of this same material, are sparingly found, and a few were included in the exhibit. Strings of similar beads are seen around the necks of sculptured figures from Mexico and Central America. It is obvious that such beads would be worn only by distinguished personages, and on state occasions.

Tubes of this slate, sometimes entire, but more frequently broken, have been gathered from all parts of the State. They are of various sizes, and many of them are as perfect as if turned in a lathe and bored with a modern drill. Unfinished specimens show that in some cases, at least, the drilling left a core after the manner of the action of a diamond drill. The drill was doubtless a node of cane, its action assisted by sand and water.

The use made of these tubes is not clear, but the words, pipe and tube, have originally the same signification, and the earliest record of tobacco smoking on the continent shows that it was done by the use of tubes. The following is quoted from a small volume entitled, "A Paper of Tobacco," "By Joseph Fume," published at London, in 1839:

"Oviedo appears to have been the earliest writer on the history of America, who mentions the word tobacco, and from the account which he gives of the *ahumadas*, or smokings of Hispaniola, we learn that the word, *tabaco*, as it is spelled by him, properly signified a smoking-tube, and not the plant nor the stupor which was the result of the Indian manner of smoking it. His chapter entitled, 'Of the Tabacos or Smokings of the Indians of the Island of Hispaniola,' appeared for the first time in the second edition, published in 1535, from which the following is quoted: "The Indians inhabiting this island have, among their other evil customs, one which is very pernicious, namely, that of smoking, called by them, *tobacco*, for the purpose of producing insensibility. This they effect by means of the smoke of a certain herb which, so far as I can learn, is of a poisonous quality, though not poisonous in appearance. * * * The manner in which they use it is as follows: The caciques and principal men have small hollowed sticks about a span long and as thick as the little finger: they are forked in the manner here shown, Y, but both the forks and the stalk are of the same piece. The forked ends are inserted in the nostrils and the other end is applied to the burning leaves of the herb, which is rolled up in the manner of pastils. They then inhale the smoke till they fall down in a state of stupor in which they remain as if intoxicated, for a considerable time. Such of the Indians as can not procure a forked stick, use a reed or hollow cane for the purpose of inhaling the smoke.'"

His descriptions show that the smoke was taken into the lungs, hence the speedy intoxication and stupor produced. This practice was evidently at first followed by Europeans, and was called *drinking* tobacco, as witness the following stanza of a moralizing tobacco-drinking poet, of the time of James I.:

> "The Indian weed withered quite,
> Green at noon, cut down at night,
> Shows thy decay—all flesh is hay,
> Thus think, then *drink* tobacco."

These quotations help to an understanding of the use of tubes for smoking, and suggest a reason for the very small bowls of very many of the pipes into which the tobacco was placed for smoking. Taken directly into the lungs, the smoke from a very small quantity would suffice.

The large, slightly trumpet-formed pipes from the Pacific Coast, described by Dr. Abbott, and the similar tubes taken by Prof. Andrews from Ohio mounds, were doubtless used for smoking, and probably substantially in the way first described by Oviedo, and if these Ohio stone tubes were used for the same purpose, they must be very old. When pipes with bowls were devised, of much easier construction, and more convenient for use, they would certainly supersede the smoking-tubes. These, as they became scarcer, might become more highly prized, and in places, be retained for sacred and ceremonial uses, as were flint knives by the Hebrews and stone axes by the Romans. Their use was, in places certainly, continued to recent times, as is evidenced by the iron mouth-piece attached to one of the specimens described by Dr. Abbott.

At the time of the construction of the Lake Shore Railroad, a pottery tube nearly of the shape and size of the largest tubes figured in Dr. Abbott's report, was taken from a mound near Collinwood, east of Cleveland. It has a highly-polished surface, simulating salt-glazing, which is probably simply the result of long use. The base gradually diminishes toward the smaller end and about three-fourths of an inch from it is much reduced by a square offset. In it when found was a slightly flattened pottery ball, which would drop down the tube until stopped by this offset. It is called a horn, and by blowing in it, a sound can be produced audible at a long distance.

The fact that a louder sound is produced when the ball is in the tube, and the mouth of the tube elevated, favors the idea that it was designed as a horn. This interesting relic belongs to F. M. Wait, of Northfield, Summit County, and was loaned by him for the exhibition.

BANNER STONES, BADGES, OR WANDS.

These are made from the slate already described, all highly polished and exhibit great varieties of form. They are too fragile to bear any very rough usage; are all of a symmetrical bilateral form, and bored at the center with great accuracy to fit them for attachment to handles. Some of them are perfect crescents, but the gradual transition from these through pick-like forms to specimens quite straight, and from these to the winged and double-crescent forms renders it improbable that any were intended to represent the crescent moon. They represent no animal forms, and the ornamental battle-axe, previously described, is the only attempt I have observed to imitate any implement of peace or war. They can not be connected with any of the symbolic forms of the old world, and if intended to be symbolical, they belong to a sealed book of human history. The clew to their significance has not been found. They were doubtless used in civil or religious ceremonies, which were held in high consideration, as is evidenced by the number and variety of the specimens found, and by the great labor expended in their production. Unfinished specimens show that large blocks were sometimes taken and carefully chipped away to a comparatively small size. Collectors of relics should remember that one rough, unfinished implement which many would throw aside as worthless, is often of more value than many highly-prized perfect specimens. It may help to a knowledge of primitive art not to be learned in any other way. The Indian picture-writing, it is believed, throws no light upon the use of these banner stones, and they probably belong to the age of the builders of the mounds, where a more dense, stationary and peaceful population and a more advanced organization would result in civic and religious ceremonials not practiced by hunting tribes. We may imagine the old priests or chiefs carrying these badges or wands in solemn procession, and of course understanding their significance, while we speculate in vain effort to understand them.

A broken specimen of one of these crescentic forms made of green gypsum, has been recently picked up in Summit County. This material is so fragile as to clearly indicate that it was intended only for ornamental or ceremonial use.

PIPES.

Smoking pipes of stone and of pottery of a great variety of forms and sizes are abundant in the State, and were well represented in the exhibit. In the State cabinet are some forty casts of elegantly carved specimens, obtained by Squire & Davis from Ohio mounds. Photographic copies of these were in the collection exhibited, and the remarkable character of the whole find is shown by the following quotation from Dr. Rau's report on the Smithsonian Archaeological Collection:

"Numerous stone pipes of a peculiar type were obtained many years ago, by Messrs. Squire & Davis, during their survey of the ancient earthworks of the State of Ohio. They have been minutely described and figured by them in the first volume of 'Smithsonian Contributions to Knowledge.' The originals of these remarkable smoking utensils (presently to be described) are now in the Blackmore Museum, at Sailsburg, England; but the National Museum possesses casts of them, which enable visitors to become acquainted with their character. These pipes were formerly thought to be chiefly made of a kind of porphyry, a substance which by its hardness would have rendered their production extremely difficult. That view, however, was erroneous, for since their transfer to the Blackmore Museum they have been carefully examined and partly analyzed by Prof. A. H. Church, who found them to consist of softer materials, such as compact slate, argillaceous iron stone, ferruginous chlorite and calcareous minerals. Nevertheless they constitute the most remarkable class of aboriginal products of art thus far discovered; for some of them are so skillfully executed that a modern artist, notwithstanding his far superior modern tools, would find no little difficulty in reproducing them.

"Four miles north of Chillicothe, Ohio, there lies close to the Sciota River, an embankment of earth somewhat in shape of a square with strongly rounded angles and enclosing an area of thirteen acres, over which twenty-three mounds are scattered, without much regularity. This work has been called "Mound City," from the great number of mounds within its precinct. In digging into the mounds, Squire & Davis discovered hearths in many of them which furnished a great number of relics, and from one of the hearths nearly two hundred stone pipes of irregular form were taken, many of which, unfortunately, were cracked by the fire or otherwise badly damaged. The occurrence of such pipes, however, was not confined to the mound in question, others having been found elsewhere in Ohio, and likewise in mounds of Indiana. In their simple, or primitive form, they present a round bowl rising from the middle of a flat and somewhat curved base, one side of which communicates by means of a narrow perforation, usually one-sixteenth of an inch in diameter, with the hollow of the bowl and represents the tube, or rather the mouth-piece of the pipe, while the other

unperforated end forms the handle by which the smoker held
the implement and approached it to his mouth. A remarkably fine specimen of this kind was found in a mound of an
ancient work in Liberty township, Ross County, (Fig. 177.)
In the more elaborate specimens from Mound City, the bowl
is formed, in a few instances, in imitation of the human
head, but generally of the body of some animal, and in the
latter cases the peculiarities of the species which have served
as models are frequently expressed with surprising fidelity.
The human heads, undoubtedly the most valuable specimens
of the series, evidently bear features characteristic of the
Indian race, and they are further remarkable for the headdress, or method of arranging the hair, (Fig. 178.) A few
of the heads show on the face incised ornamental lines,
obviously intended to imitate the painting or tattooing of
the countenance. The following animals have been recognized: The beaver, (Fig. 179;) the otter, with a fish in its
mouth, (Fig. 180;) the elk, bear, wolf, panther, wild-cat,
raccoon, opossum, squirrel and sea-cow (Manati, Lamantin,
Trichecus, manatus, Tin.) Of the animal that is supposed to
represent the sea-cow, seven carvings have been found. This
inhabitant of tropical waters is not met in the higher latitudes of North America, but only on the coast of Florida,
which is many hundred miles distant from Ohio. The
Florida Indians called this animal the "big beaver," and
hunted it on account of its flesh and bones. More frequent
are carvings of birds, among which the eagle, hawk, falcon,
turkey-buzzard, heron, (Fig. 181;) several species of owls,
the raven, swallow, parrot, duck, and other land and water
birds have been recognized. One of the specimens is supposed to represent the toucan, a tropical bird not inhabiting
the United States; but the figure is not of sufficient distinctness to identify the original that was before the artist's
mind, and it would not be safe, therefore, to make this specimen the subject of far-reaching speculations. The amphibious
(?) animals likewise have their representatives in the snake,
toad, frog, turtle and alligator. One specimen shows the

snake coiled around the bowl of the pipe. The toads, in particular, are faithful imitations of nature. Leaving aside the more than doubtful toucan, the imitated animals belong, without exception, to the North American fauna, and there is, moreover, the greatest probability that the sculptures in question were made in or near the present State of Ohio, where, in corroboration, of this view a few unfinished pipes of the described character have occurred among the complete articles.

"Pipes of this type are generally of rather small size, and in many the cavity of the bowl designed for holding the narcotic is remarkable for its insignificant capacity. These pipes were probably smoked without a stem, the narrowness of the perforations in their necks not permitting the insertion of anything thicker than a straw or a very thin reed. Yet most of the pipes of earlier date, occurring in mounds or on the surface of the ground, are provided with a hole of suitable size for the reception of a stem. A very remarkable stone pipe of this character, obtained during the survey of the Ohio earthworks by Squire & Davis, was found within an ancient enclosure twelve miles below the city of Chillicothe. It represents the body of a bird with a human head, exhibiting strongly-marked Indian features, (Fig. 182.) The original, not having been exposed to the action of the fire, is in an excellent state of preservation and retains its original beautiful polish.

"The name 'calumet pipes' has been given to large stone pipes which were smoked with a stem, and are usually fashioned in imitation of a bird, mammal or amphibian, and sometimes of the human figure. They were thus called, on account of their bulk, which seemed to indicate their character as pipes of ceremony, to be used on solemn occasions. It was further thought these pipes had not been the property of individuals, but that of communities, a view which does not seem to be altogether correct, since some have been discovered in burial mounds, accompanying a single skeleton.

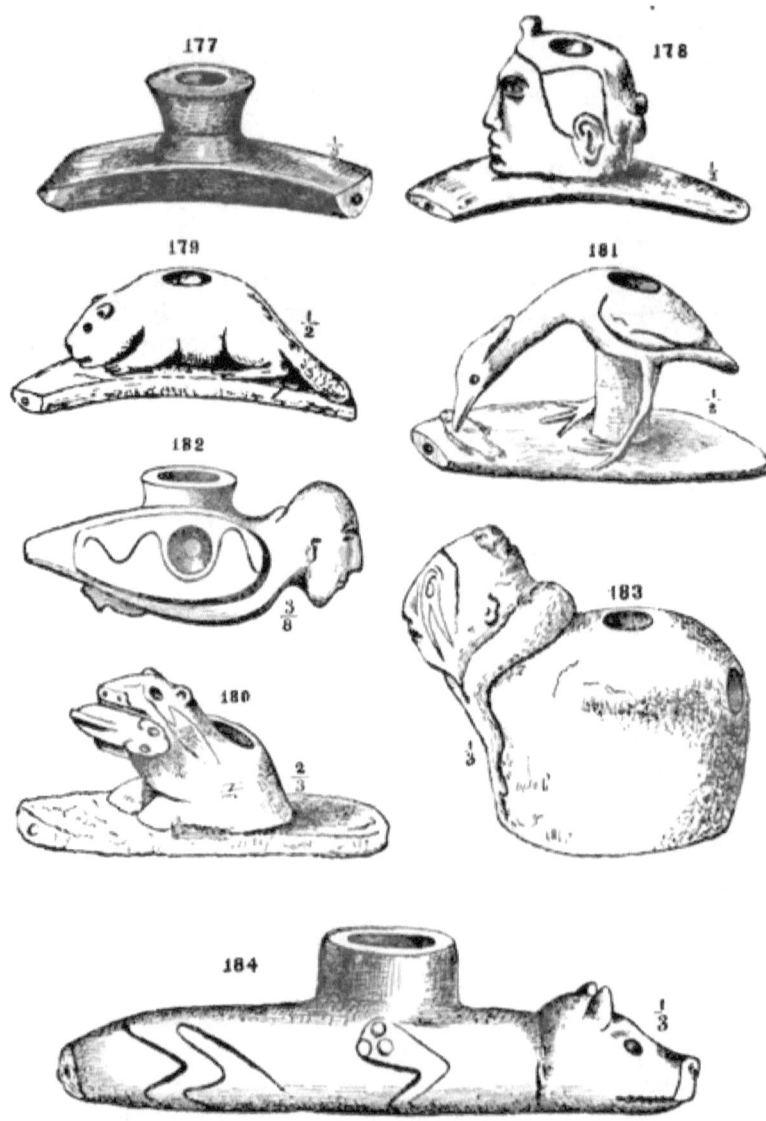

"A pipe of the kind just mentioned, is made of ferruginous sandstone, and represents, rather rudely, a human figure with a snake folded around its neck, (Fig. 183), from Paint Creek, Ross County. Another large calumet pipe, carved in imitation of a quadruped of the canine family, (probably a wolf,) consists of chlorite, and was found in Ross County."

The small size of the bowl cavities of these pipes may probably be explained by the primitive mode of smoking already described, for which a very small quantity of tobacco would suffice, and so far as we can learn the primitive use of all narcotics and intoxicants was designed not to quiet the nerves or produce a pleasurable enjoyment during their use, but to produce the complete suspension of all sensation, and as quickly as possible.

These artistically-wrought pipes from the mounds show a much higher degree of skill than was shown by the hunting tribes, indicating a higher culture on the part of the mound builders, and a greater advance toward civilization.

Among the casts in the State collection is one of a calumet pipe representing a bird, with partially expanded wings, measuring a little over nine by twelve inches. This was found in Mississippi.

Near Willoughby, in Lake County, is a site of an Indian village which has furnished a great variety of relics. A very interesting and instructive collection of pipes, finished and unfinished, was made from this locality, which is now in the Metropolitan Museum, of Central Park, New York. These show that water-worn pebbles were selected, exhibiting slightly an animal form, which the pipe-maker pecked into a more perfect animal shape without much apparent design of imitating any particular species. These were the work of modern Indians, and greatly inferior to the specimens obtained from the mounds.

Pottery pipes of various forms are more sparingly found, and one specimen only have I seen from hammered copper. Pipes of catlinite, the sacred pipe-stone of the Indians, are found, but they seem to be quite modern.

HEMATITE.

This seems to have been esteemed one of the precious stones, and was wrought by much labor into many forms. In Mr. Kinney's contribution were several highly polished small celts or axes, but whether intended as ornamental tools or for use, it is hard to determine. It contained also a very artistically-carved image of the beaver, only about one inch long, and considering the hardness of the material, perhaps the most perfect specimen of carving found in the State. It contained also several highly polished pendants or sinkers, and a number of half spheres of this material. These were worn on all sides by rubbing, and probably the abrasion of the material by rubbing furnished one of the most valued of paints. There are indications that the common Ohio iron ores were used for paint, and that the advantage of roasting them for that purpose had been learned.

In a mound at the top of a hill several hundred feet high, opened by Mr. Peter Neff, in Knox County, a considerable amount of roasted iron was found which must have been taken from the plain below.

BONE AND IRON IMPLEMENTS.

Messrs. Bauder and Baldwin exhibited a collection of bone bodkins, awls and needles, obtained from the site of the Indian village, near Willoughby, already mentioned. This place has furnished the most perfect collection of bone and horn implements of any place in the State, much of which was collected by Mr. Williams, of Chagrin Falls. Speimens of deer's horn obtained show the work of cutting instruments operating like saws by which the thickest part of the horn was cut into strips longitudinally effecting a great saving of material and adapting it to the production of small bodkins and needles. The bones of almost all animals were utilized, but mainly for the production of sharp-pointed instruments.

Mr. Kinney's collection contained many specimens of bears' teeth and claws perforated to be strung as ornaments, and several long strings of bone and shell beads; also several perfect imitations of bears' claws in cannel coal. The teeth and claws of predaceous animals seem to have been highly prized everywhere as ornaments, and were probably worn as evidence of the prowess of the hunters in overcoming these formidable animals.

COPPER IMPLEMENTS.

Col. Charles Whittlesey has collected information in regard to 720 pre-historic copper relics found in Ohio, and nearly all of these were taken from mounds. The number of specimens found in other localities is so small that we may safely assume that the manufacture of implements from this material was confined to the builders of the mounds.

It was, in their hands, a maleable stone. They did not understand the art of melting it, and casting objects from it. Laboriously hammering it into the desired forms, it was only the larger fragments that could be put to the best uses and with much waste in trimmings, that could be utilized only for beads and small ornaments.

This mode of working it developed a quality which has puzzled many archaeologists. It gave to the metal a degree of hardness which it never acquires under the ordinary mode of working it, and resulted in better cutting tools than could be made by castings unless the copper was alloyed with other metals.

Relics of this metal are so highly prized that the owners are reluctant to take the risk of sending them to distant localities, and but few specimens were exhibited. Several were exhibited by Mr. Kinney, among them a very beautiful axe in the form of a modern Indian tomahawk, the history of which was not given; but it is pretty certainly not the work of the Indians or of the mound builders.

In the collection of the Ohio University, there was a copper adz, chisel, and bodkin, taken from a small mound in Summit County, with a number of stone implements of peculiar construction, a large stone pipe, many large sheets of mica, and a large piece of galena. These articles thus grouped show a system of exchange by which articles were secured from distant localities

But a very small part of Ohio mounds have been thoroughly explored, and a completion of the explorations will doubtless increase very largely our knowledge of the prehistoric copper implements of the State.

POTTERY.

The remains of pottery in the form of fragments are very abundant in the State, while perfectly preserved vessels are comparatively rare. They are all of coarse character, imperfectly burned, and generally composed of clay and powdered shell. Specimens obtained from a rock shelter in Summit County, show the use of powdered quartz pebbles of the adjacent carboniferous conglomerate, mixed with clay. These exhibit markings on the outside such as would be produced by beating the inner bark of the basswood, macerated in water, until the fibres were crushed and separated, and using this as lining to a cavity or model to be plastered with the prepared clay. The upper margin is generally turned outward and pierced with holes for handles, made while the material was soft and plastic. An entire vessel from the collection of the Fire Lands Historical Society, of Norwalk, exhibited at Philadelphia, indicates the use of grass as a lining to the mold in which it was formed.

There were two perfect vessels in Mr. Kinney's collection in New Orleans, one in the form of a small basin, the other a large vase.

The forms and texture of the pottery from all parts of the Mississippi Valley, are very much alike, but with an increased tendency to the west and southwest to adopt the human and animal forms so abundant in New Mexico. Specimens obtained in Ohio are mostly found in rock shelters and in mounds.

The earliest manufactured vessels everywhere were of pottery, and the study of ancient ceramic art is especially interesting to the archaeologist. Similar forms are found everywhere, and are often continued in more costly material. In many instances these forms can be traced back to the time when all vessels were formed of natural products. The delicate long-necked bottles or vases, now made of Bohemian glass, are substantially of the same form as the orthodox whiskey bottle of forty years ago; are exact copies in glass of the pottery water coolers now made in India, Africa and South America, of which many specimens were exhibited at Philadelphia, and which are found in the earliest collections of pottery known. All are imitations of the earliest bottle used—the gourd with its long neck. The Rhyton, brought to the Greeks from Egypt, and of which substantially similar forms were exhumed by Schlieman, perpetuated by the Greeks and Romans in silver and other costly material, was a drinking cup which could not be set down until its contents were emptied. Its origin is clearly preserved in its name, "drinking horn," and its use, in the slang phrase, "taking a horn;" and the practice still preserved in many places in drinking bouts of reversing the cup upon the table as an indication that it is empty. Originally it was a veritable horn which could stand only in a reversed position. The ancient vases found in America, in pottery, and in Europe in silver and other costly material, with small rounded bases which required tripods for their support, would never have taken such forms as original inventions. They were imitations of vases made from the shells of nuts and other natural productions. Hence similar forms found in widely separated localities, do not indicate community of race or commercial intercourse, but that man everywhere was at first dependent upon natural productions, which he adapted to his wants, and afterward imitated, and gradually modified their forms.

SHELLS.

Fresh and salt water shells were largely utilized by the primitive inhabitants of the State. The sharp edges of the fresh water muscles made them valuable as knives and scrapers, and the contents of mounds show that they were used as spoons, cups for holding paint and other articles. From the large salt-water univalves they made excellent dippers, and inscribed circular ornamental disks which were apparently worn upon the breast and were often buried with the dead. They were favorite material for the beads, of which many are found preserved in graves, and would naturally be used for a variety of purposes, some of which may not be apparent to us.

ROCK SHELTERS.

Caves adapted to human habitation are very rare in Ohio, but rock shelters, which would afford protection from the weather, are abundant. These have been very inadequately explored. Every rocky projection under which a benighted hunter would seek protection, if there is a dry surface below it, will, on examination, show evidences of human habitation, and sometimes of a habitation greatly prolonged. Such a rock shelter in Summit County, already referred to, was explored by me some years ago, and a description contributed to the *American Antiquarian*. As this may be regarded as a typical rock shelter, and a description of it may lead to other explorations, the greater part of the communication to the *Antiquarian* is here copied:

"In the eastern part of Boston township, the outcrop of the carboniferous conglomerate exhibits bold bluffs, fissured with ravines, with large masses of detached rocks at the base of the bluffs, where the rock has been undermined, and broken by its own weight, or else detached and pushed out of place by the ice. So-called caves, which are simply long fissures in the rocks, are abundant, often with springs of pure water at the bottom, while the margin and detached rocks afford shelters which would be attractive places for residences to those unable to build comfortable dwellings. Among these detached rocks is one shelter composed of two large blocks, twenty or more feet in diameter, separated about fifteen feet with a huge block resting upon the top at the height of about twelve feet, making a large, perfectly protected room, open only at the north and south, and the northern opening perfectly protected from storms by its close proximity to the adjacent bluff. Such a rock shelter it is evident would afford a much better family dwelling than could be easily erected without good cutting tools, and would certainly be occupied by people having the characteristics of our native races. The abundant springs of water, the abundance of game to be found in this wood-covered, broken region, not far from the Cuyahoga River, which was one of their channels of communication, would be sure to attract occupants.

"The exploration of this shelter was made in the early part of June, 1878. After removing a few inches of vegetable mold, a mixture of ashes and earth was reached extending to the depth of from four and a half to five feet at the bottom, filling fissures and covering rock fragments which originally rested on the floor of the cave, and which the occupants did not attempt to remove. These scattered blocks covered the sandy debris of the conglomerate and were gradually buried beneath the accumulated deposits of ashes and dirt, the evidences of long-continued occupancy.

"The whole of this material was filled with evidences of the use of the place as a human residence—pottery, bones, shells, and stone implements. In the deposit of these there was no sudden transition. The bones near the top were in a good state of preservation; those that had not been changed by the fire, not blackened, but colored slightly yellow by lapse of time. They became darker and less abundant as the excavation was carried deeper, and substantially disappeared before the bottom of the excavation was reached, showing that the earliest occupancy was so long ago that the bones in the dry shelter had been consumed by time.

"Over two hundred and fifty fragments of pottery were collected. This had been manufactured in the immediate neighborhood, for it was composed of clay in which had been mixed coarsely pulverized fragments of the quartz pebbles of the conglomerate. It was all coarse without any attempt at ornamentation for the sake of ornament. The outside of most of it and the inside of a part of it was minutely marked by sharply-defined depressions or casts, not the marks of basket work or braided grass, but such as would be produced if a mold for the formation of a vessel had been lined with the macerated and beaten bark of the elm or basswood. The mode of manufacture indicated is as follows: A cavity was formed in earth or sand, of the form of the outside of the vessel; a coating of bark was prepared by macerating in water, beating it with stones until the fibers were partially separated, and the whole mass rendered soft and plastic. With this the cavity was lined and then plastered with the prepared clay. After it had sufficiently dried, the whole was lifted out of the mould and ultimately burned in the fire. In other cases a mold was formed of the form of the inside of the proposed vessel, covered with bark, and the clay plastered upon the outside of it. This of course results in leaving the bark markings on the inside of the vessel.

"Three forms of the rim or upper edge of the vessels were observed, one terminating abruptly without any curve, or angle; one with an outer angle about three-fourths of an inch from the margin, and one with a regular outward curve. Small holes were made in the pottery, when soft, near the edge of the rim, and in one fragment a hole had been drilled of a conical form, after it was burned, probably—certainly after it was dry. The pottery near the bottom of the excavation was less abundant, heavier and coarser, but made in a similar manner.

"The stone implements were abundant, but most of them rude and coarse, only eleven flint or chert implements, and among these two small perfect arrow points, one fragment of a spear or knife, two scrapers and one rimmer; the others were flakes or irregular fragments.

"There was one fragment of a polished stone implement. This was the bit of a flat-sided celt or gouge, which was of especial interest from the fact that it had been broken at the edge, and repaired by bringing the nicked part down to an edge; this was done by pecking out the substance of the stone in a groove running back a little over an inch till a new edge was obtained by a depression in the bit. The repaired portion was not polished.

"There was one fragment of a polished granite hammer, several water-worn boulders, evidently gathered for hammerstones, fourteen flakes from conglomerate pebbles, and sixteen from water-worn drift pebbles. Both of these materials were utilized by striking a slice from one side, which would naturally produce a cutting edge on the side opposite to that on which the breaking force was applied. Oblate forms of these pebbles were selected, as they would yield a better shaped flake. One wrought but unfinished stone implement was found of the form called by some, 'shuttles,' but unpolished and without perforations. It was from the material of the local shales.

"The most abundant of the stone implements were cutting tools or knives. Of these, seventy-five were gathered, made from the local shales and the shales of the drift. They were all primitive forms of the stone knife, the material split in such manner as to secure a cutting edge, with the least labor, and without any attempt to secure any particular form, some showing that after the cutting edge had been dulled by use, it was sharpened by blows upon the edge.

"Besides these there were about twenty rock fragments apparently broken out for rude scrapers or as a material from which to make cutting tools.

"All showed a meagre supply of material, and but very slight skill in adapting it to use. The great bulk of the material was from the immediate neighborhood, the pebbles of the conglomerate and of the drift and the shales which crop out in the valley.

"Not a single article was found designed for ornament, nor was there any attempt to ornament any of the articles found. Everything seemed adapted to the necesssities of the lowest savage life.

"The relative proportions of the different kinds of implements, and the fact that the most of those of polished stone and chert were fragments, and the mode of repairing one of these fragments, indicate that the crude forms alone were of home production, while the others were either picked up from the ground, or obtained from other tribes.

"An abundance of bone fragments indicated the large use of animal food. Every shaft-bone, and the lower jaws of all the larger animals were so broken that every particle of the marrow could be extracted, and there was a rude attempt to fashion a few of the bone fragments into useful forms. Over a half-bushel of these fragments was collected, and from the meagre supply of materials for tools, it was quite remarkable that no more use was made of these fragments.

"Among the bones could be identified those of the bear, the wolf, the beaver, the hedgehog, the deer, the buffalo, the raccoon, the skunk, the chipmunk and the fox. There were a number of the bones of birds, of which those of the turkey and large blue herron were probably identified. A number of mussel shells from the Cuyahoga were also found. In the fragments of the jaws and in the whole jaws the teeth were ordinarily in place, showing no attempt to use these as ornaments or otherwise. The fire seemed to have been built near the center of the shelter, and the bulk of the bone fragments were found upon the west side, and of the pottery upon the east, showing the ordinary savage division of labor, the care of the cooked food being given to those on one side of the shelter and that of the cooking and cooking utensils to those occupying the other side. It is not difficult to imagine that the latter was the quarter of the women."

HUMAN EFFIGIES.

Effigies of the human face and figure, carved in stone, are abundant in Ohio relics. An entire figure in a sitting position laboriously worked out of granite and with marked Indian features, was exhibited by Mr. Kinney, and called an "Idol," but there is no evidence that it deserves that name, unless it is used in its primitive sense, meaning simply an image and not suggesting any religious worship. Children and savages everywhere make early attempts to delineate the human figure, and with results remarkably similar. Attempts to carve the human figure soon follow the attempt, involving greater labor, but producing much more satisfactory results, for savage artistic skill is never equal to giving any roundness or projection to a drawing. A pretended savage drawing that attempts to do this may pretty safely be set down as a fraud and the work of one who has learned something of the laws of perspective.

Several images have been obtained from Stark County, one a grotesque figure carved in variegated marble and represented as obtained in sinking a well and at the depth of twelve feet, and below a stratum of very compact yellow clay. It was discovered in a bucket of boulders when brought to the surface from the bottom of the well, and believed by all present to be taken from the bottom. If really found in such a place, it would carry back the life of the sculptor to the age of the drift. All who have seen it seem to have no doubt of its being a work of art, but its very crude character, as shown by an engraving from a photograph, suggests the possibility that the form is the result of accident. (A wood-cut of this image is here introduced.)

The probabilities are so much against the finding of a carved image in such a position, that it would be more reasonable to suppose, if a genuine carving, that it was loosened from the soil near the surface, and dropped without being observed into the well.

A few years ago, workmen, in digging a well, in Hudson, brought up from a depth of about eighty feet in compact blue drift clay, a live frog, which they were sure they dug out at that depth. One of its legs had been cut off apparently by a mowing machine. Its life in the well was evidently measured by a part of the time between cessation of work in the evening, and the commencement of work in the morning.

Quite an artistically carved head in sandstone was dug up while opening the Sandy & Beaver Canal, in Columbiana County, which now belongs to J. F. Benner & Son, of New Lisbon, a cut of which is here given; and a carving in sandstone picked up on the surface in Norristown, Carroll County, now in the cabinet of G. G. B. Greenwood, of Minerva, shows characteristic Indian features. These are illustrated in a pamphlet published by Col. Charles Whittlesey.

Many other carvings of images and faces have been collected, but none of them have any special significance, except a single specimen to be hereafter described. They do not exhibit that degree of artistic skill which would make them reliable evidence of race or tribal characteristics. They show how much work, with poor tools, was expended in the production of images, having no form or comeliness to make them worthy of admiration, but which were doubtless esteemed by the artists and their contemporaries as remarkable triumphs of artistic skill.

Mr. Peter Neff, of Gambier, has a mask-like face, carved in sandstone, which was plowed up in a field in Jackson township, Coshocton County, in 1851. It measures $3\frac{1}{4} \times 2\frac{3}{4}$ inches, not including two projections or blunt horns rising on each side of the top of the head. It is of especial interest from its close resemblance to similar faces worn on the breast of priest-like personages represented on Central American sculptures, of which illustrations are given by Bancroft in his "Native Races of the Pacific States." In his illustrations these face-ornaments are in one instance suspended by a string of very large beads, apparently quite similar to the large metamorphic slate beads found in this State, and previously described.

The projections from the top of Mr. Neff's specimen were plainly intended for purposes of suspension, and if suspended from a string of these large Ohio beads the whole would be a complete repetition of the ornament figured by Bancroft. A precisely similar face, except having only one projection from the top of the head, has been found in Missouri. A cut 3-5 size of Mr. Neff's specimen is here inserted.

FIRE HEARTHS.

In all parts of the State are found hearths formed of rough stones, laid snugly side by side, and generally several feet square. They are usually in groups, and show the long-continued action of fire. They are the sites of ancient village communities and encampments, and the abundance of relics about them indicate long-continued occupancy. Along the banks of the Ohio, above Portsmouth, Mr. Thomas W. Kinney has found such hearths, disclosed by the encroachment of the river, which are now six and eight feet beneath the surface; and Col. Whittlesey reports such hearths fifteen feet below the surface, indicating very great antiquity.

PICTURE-WRITING AND INSCRIBED ROCKS.

Col. Charles Whittlesey, of Cleveland, Ohio, has given more attention to the study of these remains than any other man in the State, and by his permission the following extracts from a chapter on ancient rock sculptures, prepared by him for the Centennial report, are here copied:

"In many places within the State rude effigies of man and animals have been observed, chiseled or picked into the natural surface of the rocks. They are most numerous in the eastern half of the State, where the grits of the coal series furnish large blocks or perpendicular faces of sandrock, which are easily cut, and which are, at the same time, imperishable. These surfaces are never prepared for inscriptions by artificial smoothing. The figures are sunk into the stone by some sharp-pointed tool like a pick, which has left the impression of its point similar to the rough-hewn stone of our masonry. This tool has not been found in the form of a pick, and was probably only a small angular stone, held in the hand and used as a chipper until the points and angles were worn off. Many artificial stones of flint, trap, and greenstone are seen in all large collections, from two to four inches in diameter, evidently worn into a partially rounded form by blows that have chipped off the projecting corners. Some are quite thoroughly rounded and even polished like the spherical balls. Such balls, sometimes called "slingstones" or "slung-shots," could, in their rough condition, have answered the purpose of a picking tool, at the same time being itself brought into shape for a weapon or an ornament. Such contrivances, to save labor by accomplishing two purposes at once, are visible in other fabrications of the early races. Rude picks of the early races in Europe have been found, which were made by inserting a pointed stone in the prong of a deer's horn. Such an implement seems to be required to finish some of the channeling observed on some of our rocks, and may yet be found. How ancient the intaglios are can not yet be determined, but there is one instance at Independence, Cuyahoga County, where soil had accumulated over them to a depth of one to one and a half feet, on which were growing trees of the usual size in that region. The Western Reserve Historical Society has procured several tracings of them on muslin, of the size of nature, which were forwarded for exhibition.

"It has been found that sketches, even by good artists, are so deficient in accuracy as to be of little value. By clearing out the channels sunk in the rock, painting them heavily, and pressing a sheet of muslin into the freshly-painted depressions, an exact outline is obtained. This is photographed to the size intended for engraving, and thus the reduced copy remains an accurate *fac simile* of the original. Those which are mentioned below were traced and reduced in this manner.

"Track Rocks Near Barnesville, Belmont County, Ohio.

"In 1857 or 1858, Mr. Thomas Kite, of Cincinnati, examined the 'track rocks' near Barnesville, and took casts of some of the sculptured figures. Jas. W. Ward, Esq., of the same city, soon afterward made a detailed sketch, which he caused to be engraved and circulated. In 1869 Dr. J. Salisbury and myself made a visit to the place with a view to get a tracing on cloth, but were compelled to give it up for want of time. An arrangement was made with Dr. Jas. W. Walton, of Barnesville, to take tracing for this Society, which, however, was not received until the fall of 1871. The discussion which took place at the Indianapolis meeting of the American Association, in August, 1871, was based upon Mr. Ward's sketch, which had been made with much care, he being not only an artist but an antiquarian.

"This was reproduced, with a detailed description, by Mr. Ward, in the first number of the *American Anthropological Journal*, issued in January, 1872, at New York. When Dr. Walton's *fac simile* tracings, size of nature, were received, it was evident that notwithstanding the care exercised by Mr. Ward, there were important omissions, which destroyed the value of the discussions at Indianapolis, based upon his sketch. It is now conceded that copies of such sculptures must be made by casts, squeezes, or tracings, in order to be reliable. In the different representations that have appeared of the 'Dighton Rock,' the supposed Grave Creek stone, the 'Big Indian Rock,' on the Susquehanna, and the 'Independence Stone,' of this county, something material is omitted, or palpably distorted. Mere sketches are of little or no ethnological value. I think the mode adopted by us leaves little room for errors, either in size or proportion, but there may be in the manner or aspect that belongs to every object, and which is known by the plain but forcible expression, 'lifelike.' The rock was first thoroughly cleaned of the moss and dirt, as Dr. Walton explains in his letter accompanying the tracings. All of the artificial depressions were then filled with paint, and a sheet of muslin, covering the entire block, pressed into the sculptured figures. This coarse grit is so nearly imperishable that whatever distinct markings were originally cut upon it are doubtless there now and are not perceptibly injured by exposure. These groups present the first instance among the rock inscriptions of Ohio, where it can be said that we now have complete and entire, in their primitive condition, all the figures that are capable of being traced, not mutilated by man, or obliterated by the elements. Dr. Walton's description will now be both intelligible and interesting:

"'The copies I send you exhibit every definite figure those rocks contain, and indeed many more than will be noticed by a casual observer of them.

"'Some of them were discovered only after removing the lichens of ages; others after glancing the eye along the surface of the rocks from every point of the compass; and others after the sun had declined low in the west, casting dim shadows over depressions too shallow to be seen before. And there are many indistinct impressions on each of the rocks that could not be copied— these resemble the indefinite remains of innumerable tracks of men and animals, overlying each other, as may be seen on our highways, after a rain has effaced almost every outline.

"'Upon examining the print of the smaller rock it will appear that two men, each accompanied by a dog, seem to have passed over it in opposite directions. This idea has never, so far as I have learned, occurred to any person who has heretofore examined the rocks; the figures being regarded as distinct and disconnected, as they appear on the larger stone. I did not catch the idea until after I had painted all the distinct figures on this stone, and had impressed the cloth on the paint, when, upon removing and examining the print, I found, say, first a right foot print, then a left one at its appropriate position, then a right foot where it should be, but the succeeding left one wanting.

"'This set me on a more careful examination of the motley indentations covering this part of the rock for traces of the lost feet, and it was not a great while before I found sufficient remains of just what was wanting, and at their appropriate places, but in exceedingly indistinct impressions.

"'The rude cuts of human faces, part of the human feet, the rings, stars, serpents, and some others are evidently works of art, as in the best of them the marks of the engraving instrument are to be seen; and it is barely possible that the residue of those figures were carved by the hands of men; however, I must say that the works of the best sculptors do not surpass the equisite finish of most of the tracks on those rocks.'"

"PLATE I.—BARNESVILLE TRACK ROCKS NO. 1—1-20TH OF NATURE.

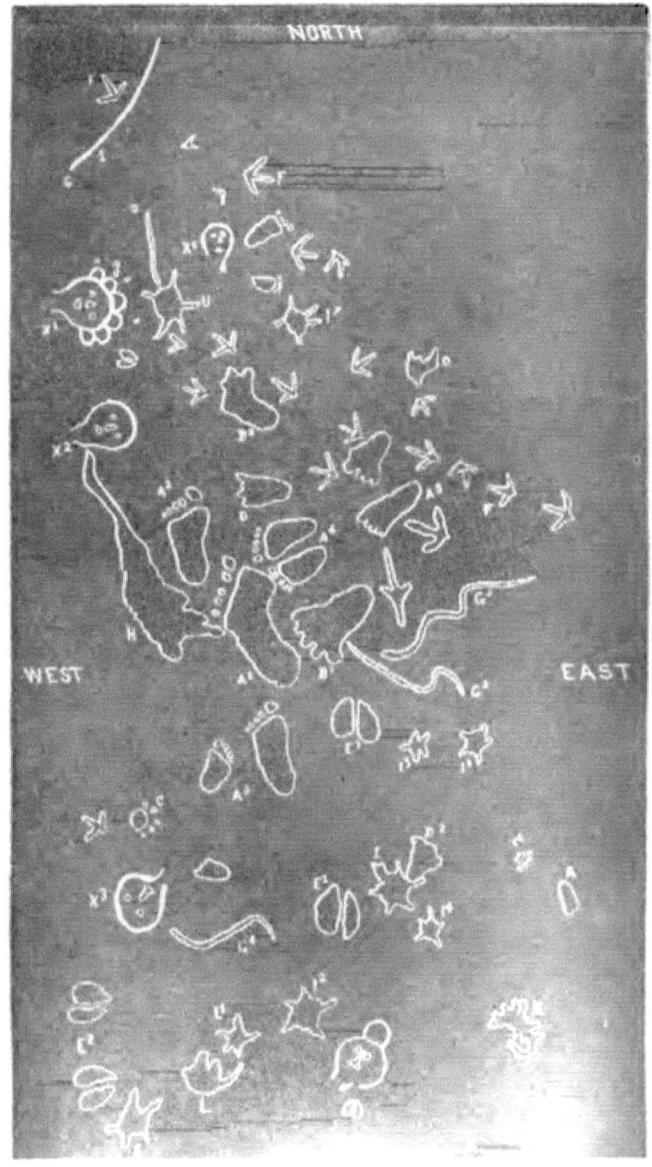

"PLATE II.—ENLARGED FIGURES OF NO. 1—1-7TH OF NATURE.

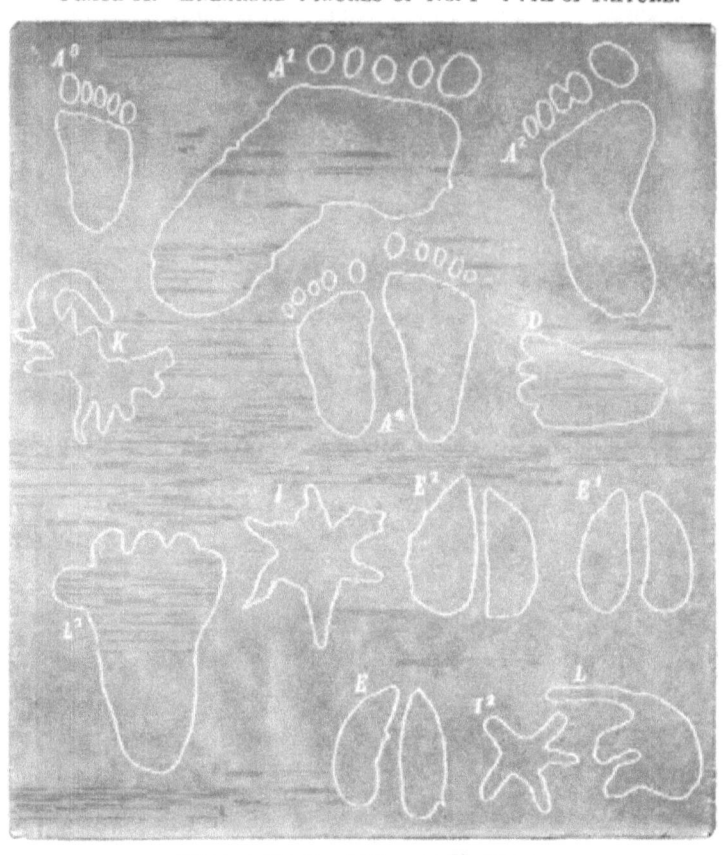

"BLOCK NO. 1.—1-20TH OF NATURE.

"In all cases, whether single or in groups, the relative dimensions of the figures are preserved. The surface of this block is eight by eleven feet. An error has crept into the engraving of this group, in regard to the east and west sides, which should be reversed: for east read west, and for west, east.

"a^1—human foot, greatest length 15 inches.
"a^2—human foot, greatest length 10 inches.
"a^6—human foot, greatest length 3½ inches.
"b—Nos. 1 and 2, awparently the fore foot of a bear, 5½ to 9 inches long.
"c—hind foot of a wolf or dog, breadth across the toes 3½ inches.
"c^1—hind foot of a wolf or dog, breadth across the toes 2½ inches.
"d—probably the hind foot of a bear, length 5½ inches.
"e—Nos. 1 to 5, buffalo tracks, length 2 to 5 inches.
"f—Nos. 1 to 13, so called 'bird tracks,' 3½ to 5 inches in length.
"g—Nos. 1 to 4, snakes, or portions of them, 13 to 21 inches in length.
"h—effigy of a bird, greatest length 22 inches.
"i—Nos. 1 to 9 resembles the spread out skin of an animal, 3 to 8 inches greatest diameter.
"k—not recognized as an animal form, length 6 inches.
"l—an imperfect figure.
"n—probably a variation of i, with a groove that may have been part of the figure.
"o—apparently incomplete.
"p—greatest length 6 inches.
"q—spirit circle, diameter 7½ inches.
"x—Nos. 1 to 3, outlines of the human face, breadth 3½ to 6 inches.

"There is a rock in Georgia, described by the antiquarian, C. C. Jones, of that State, on which are a number of circles like 'g,' a sign used by the Chippeways to represent a spirit.

—72—

"Plate III.—Barnesville Track Rock No. 2—1-19 and 1-7 of Nature.

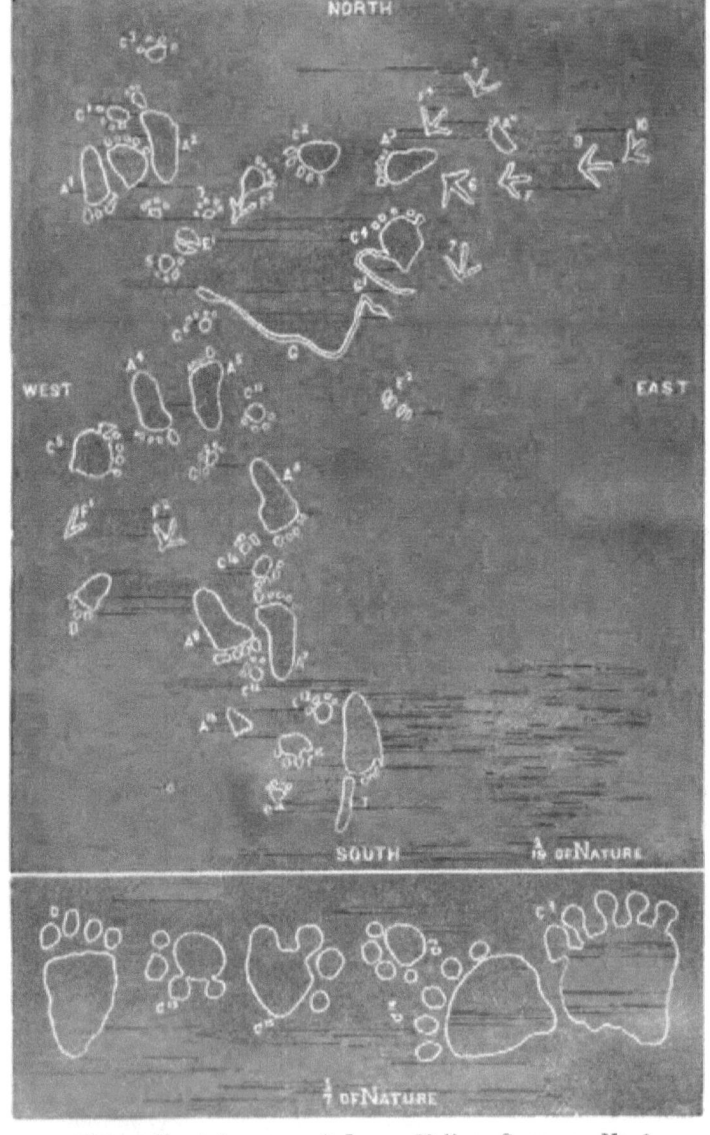

"Block No. 2, 7 feet by 8. Lying 20 feet South of No. 1.

"a—Nos. 2, 6, 7, and 8, human foot 9 inches long.
"a¹⁰—human foot 3½ inches long.
"c—Nos. 1 and 10 to 16, hind foot of a dog or wolf, 2½ to 4 inches broad across the toes.
"e—Nos. 2, 3, 4, and 5, five toes, greatest breadth 4 to 5½ inches across the toes (the animal not recognized.)
"d—hind foot of a bear.
"e¹—buffalo track, 3 inches long.
"e²—buffalo track 1½ inches long, a pair.
"f—so-called "bird tracks," 3½ to 5 inches long.
"g—snake, 21 inches long; g¹—part of same.
"i—groove, 5 inches long.

"We have here as good representations as it is possible to procure of an entire rock inscription. The copy of the Independence stone embraces only a fragment of the original, not exceeding one-fourth of the surface once covered with sculptured effigies. If the figures had a general relation to each other, it could not be determined by an inspection of only a portion of them.

"The inscriptions near Newark, in Licking County, Ohio, originally covered a vertical face of conglomerate rock, fifty or sixty feet in length, by six and eight feet in height. This rock is soft, and, therefore, the figures are easily erased. As the place was partially sheltered from the weather by overhangs, the injury done to them by exposure was not much; but from the earliest settlement of the country, about the year 1800, it became a place where white men sought to immortalize themselves by cutting their names across the old inscriptions. When Dr. Salisbury, in 1864, undertook to rescue what remained of them, it was only possible to trace the ancient figures over a space about seven feet by thirteen, and here many of them were restored with difficulty, by great patience and labor. His copy is in the hands of the American Antiquarian Society, and is in the course of publication. It is, therefore, like the Independence stone, only a fragment.

"On the rock-faces and detached sandstone blocks of the banks of the Ohio River, there are numerous groups of intaglios, but in them the style is quite different from those to which I have referred, and which are located in the interior. Those on the Ohio River resemble the symbolical records of the North American Indians, such as the Kelley Island stone, described in Schoolcraft by Captain Eastman, the Dighton Rock, the Big Indian Rock of the Susquehanna, and the 'God Rock' of the Alleghany River. In those the supposed bird track is generally wanting. The large sculptured rock, near Wellsville, which is only visible at low water of the Ohio, has among the figures one that is prominent on the Barnesville stones. This is the fore foot of the bear, with the outside toe distorted and set outward at right angles.

"PLATE IV.—INDEPENDENCE SLAB, 4½ BY 6 FEET, NOW IN THE WEST WALL OF THE CHURCH—1-14TH OF NATURE.

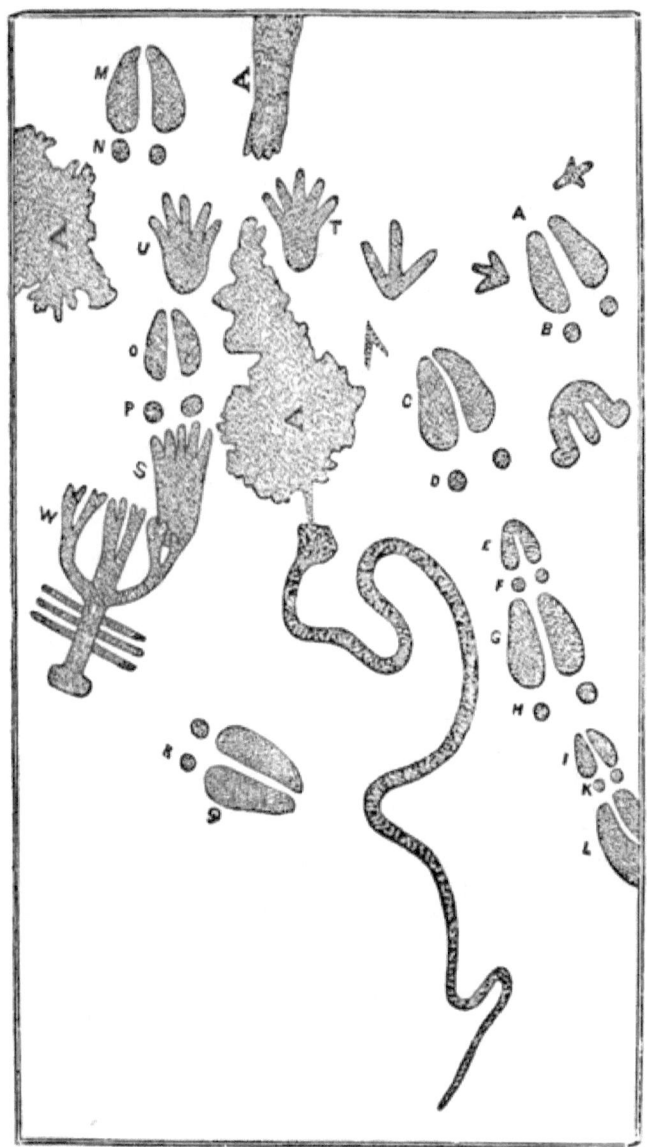

"A A A—Irregular patches slightly worked with a pick.

"THE INDEPENDENCE STONE.

"Great care has been taken to obtain a correct sketch of what remains of this inscription. A very rude drawing of it was published in Schoolcraft's great work upon the Indian tribes, in 1854. He probably regarded it as the work of the red man. In 1869, Dr. J. H. Salisbury, who has long been engaged in the investigation of rock inscriptions at the West, in company with Dr. Lewis, of the Asylum at Newburgh, made a copy, by means of full and exact measurements.

"As no sketch is of equal authenticity with a photograph, Mr. Thos. T. Sweeney, an artist at Cleveland, went to Independence, and took a copy with his instrument. The light on that day was not favorable, but the outlines of all the artificial work upon the stone were thus secured with exactness. For the purposes of the engraver, the figures were filled in by Dr. Salisbury from his sketch. Without expressing an opinion as to the authors of these inscriptions, I present, in connection with the engraving, the details furnished by Dr. Salisbury:

"'Mr. W. F. Bushnell, who resides at Independence, and M. B. Wood, of Cleveland, state that these markings were discovered about 1853, while stripping the earth from the surface of a quarry on the north brow of the hill on which the village of Independence stands. Here the rocks projected in the form of a perpendicular cliff, from twenty to forty feet in height. On the top of this cliff, and near its edge, the markings were discovered. The soil over the markings was from five to eight inches in depth, and was black, having been formed from decaying vegetation. A tree was growing directly over the markings, that was one foot or more in diameter. Within a few feet of the spot there was an oak tree over four feet in diameter. This tree, some years previous to the discovery of the sculptured rock, had fallen nearly across the markings, and, in 1853, was much decayed. Besides the markings represented in the engraving, there were others adjacent, belonging to the same group, which had been destroyed by the quarrymen before Messrs. Bushnell and Wood were aware of it. Among the markings destroyed, were the outline figures of a man and woman, very well executed. There were also the representations of a wolf's foot, and figures of the feet of other animals.

"'At the time of the discovery the stone church at Independence was being built, and, at the suggestion of Deacon Bushnell and others, all the markings not previously destroyed were carefully cut out, and the block placed in the rear wall of the church, about eight feet above the ground. It was prudently placed at this height to prevent its being defaced, for they are not very distinct.

"'In company with Dr. Lewis. Superintendent of the Northern Ohio Lunatic Asylum, I visited the locality on the 5th day of June, 1869, and made careful drawings of all the markings visible on the block in the rear wall of the church. These, with accurate measurements, are represented here, made more perfect by the use of Mr. Sweeney's photography.

"'The rock here described only contains a portion of the inscription; the balance was destroyed in quarrying. The markings on the portion of the rock preserved consist of the human foot, clothed with something like a moccasin or stocking; of the naked foot; of the open hand; of round markings, one in front of the great toe of each representation of the clothed foot; the figure of a serpent; and peculiar character w, which might be taken for rude representation of a crab or crawfish, but which bears a closer resemblance to an old-fashioned spear head, used in capturing fish.

"'The clothed feet are of five different sizes. There are eighteen impressions of this kind, arranged in nine pairs. Of the largest size there are five pairs—a, c, g, l, m; of the next size smaller there is only one pair—o; of the next smaller size one pair—g; of the next smaller size one pair—c; of the next smaller size one pair. Of the naked foot there is only a single figure, which is rudely carved, and which is much longer than the clothed representations. There are two figures of the open hand— one with a large palm and short fingers, the other smaller, with fingers long and slender.

"'The sculptures have all been made with a sharp-pointed instrument, by the process of pecking, and sunk in throughout instead of being mere outlines. The cuttings are from one-eighth to half an inch deep. The two hands are sculptured the deepest. In the illustrations I have endeavored to give an idea of the markings left by the tool used, though these are less evident than the representations.

"'The length of the largest feet in figures $a, c, g, l, m,$ from the extremity of the great toe to the heel, is six and three-fourths inches, and the width, at the widest place, two and three-fourths inches. The length of the next in size, o, is five inches, and the width two and one-eighth inches; and of g, five inches by two inches. Length of next smaller size, c, three and a half inches, and width one and three-fourths inches, and three and three-fourths inches by one and a half inches. The length of the naked foot, s, is nine inches, and greatest width, four and three-fourths inches. The great toe is one inch long, the second toe one and one-fourth inches long, the third toe one and a half inches long, the fourth toe one and a fourth inches long, and the little toe one inch long.

"'In the large hand, t, the palm is five and a half inches long and three and a half inches wide. The length of the thumb is one and a half inches, the index finger one and three-fourths inches, the middle finger two inches, the ring finger one and three-fourths inches, and the little finger one and a half inches. In the other hand, *u*, the palm is three and a half inches long and two and a half inches wide. The length of the thumb is two and one-fourth inches, the index finger two and a half inches, the middle finger two and three-fourths inches, the ring finger two and a fourth inches, and the little finger two inches.

"'The diameter of the circular markings, invariably found in front of the clothed feet, are as follows: *b*, one and one-eighth inches; *d*, one and three-fourths inches; *f*, three-fourths inch; *h*, one inch; *k*, half inch; *n*, one and a half inches; *p*, one and one-fourth inches; *q*, one inch.

"'The diameter of the serpent's head is two and three-fourths inches; length of body, ninety-four inches, making the entire length of the figure about eight feet.

"'In the sculptured figure, *w*, the measurements are omitted.

"'It is evident this slab does not contain the entire description. The tracks, *l*, are only partially present, while it is very probable that more tracks occurred in the direction *a*, *b*, arranged in a line as those are from *c* to *l*, where there are ten tracks and eight round characters, and which are probably not all that were originally in this line previous to the stones being quarried. The round markings in front of the clothed tracks may have been intended to represent the track of dogs or wolves, but at present they are so smoothed by time that it is impossible to make out anything but simple irregular circular depressions.

"'The rock on which the inscription occurs is the grindstone grits of the Ohio Reports, an extensive stratum in Northern Ohio, about one hundred and fifty feet below the conglomerate. It is almost pure silex, and possesses the property of resisting atmospheric changes to a remarkable degree. Boulders and projecting portions of the formation, from which this block was obtained, that have been exposed to the weather for ages, preserve perfectly their sharp, angular projections. As a building stone it is superior on account of its extreme durability. This durability of the rock, and the fact that these markings were covered with earth, explains why they have been so finely preserved.

"'The markings *a*, *c*, *e*, *g*, *l*, *m*, *o*, and *q*, have been supposed by some to represent the tracks of the buffalo. After carefully measuring them, however, I have come to the conclusion that they were designed to represent tracks of the clothed human foot, and as such have described them.

"'The so-called bird tracks, which are few and faint on this slab, are numerous and bold on most of the rock inscriptions of Ohio.'"

It is difficult to determine whether any of these sculptures can be properly called picture writings. There is no regular order of arrangement; no systematic grouping of characters pointing to a serial connection between them. In a specimen of modern Indian picture-writing, purporting to be the life of a Chippeway, and deposited in the Museum of the Natural Science Association, of Detroit, the characters are arranged in regular order, there being two series on each side of a wooden tablet, the feet of the figures of men and animals directed toward the edge of the tablet, clearly indicating a methodical arrangement, and that the record is to be read from one end to the other, along one series of characters, when the other edge of the tablet was to be turned upward and the reading continued to the place of beginning. It is not apparent whether the reading should be from right to left or the reverse, nor where the reading should begin. It is certainly a much more perfect specimen of picture-writing than any of the rock inscriptions in Ohio, and all of the latter are probably the work of modern Indians.

EARTH WORKS.

The ancient earth works of Ohio, in their variety, magnitude and extent, excel those of all the other States. Single mounds of greater size are found elsewhere, but no other State has such a variety of these works, or such numbers of them as Ohio. When it is remembered that the builders of these works had no beasts of burden, or draught, no metal tools of a size or character to be of any use in their construction; that all the material must have been laboriously carried to its place in baskets, it will be obvious that the real labor expended upon some of them was not much, if any, less than that expended upon the largest pyramid of Egypt. Such works could be constructed only by a people who had a compact, civil organization, with a central authority which could control the labor of the masses, and with dominant civil or religious ideas which would induce the masses to submit to long-continued labor. The more extensive works peculiar to the State, indicate large, fixed communities, which involves the practice of agriculture and habits of life very different from that of the hunting tribes, roaming over the State, upon its first occupancy by the whites.

The most of these works are confined to the valleys of the streams where there is land specially adapted to the cultivation of maize or Indian corn, which was the basis of pre-Columbian American agriculture. They are much more abundant in the northern and southern than in the central parts of the State, a fact which might be easily explained from the small extent of the alluvial valley, on the table and. Still there is a marked difference in the character of those in the northern and southern regions. The former have more the appearance of defense works, both in their location and mode of construction. They ordinarily occupy elevated spurs, projecting from the table land into the valleys, overlooking extensive alluvial plains—often where erosion has left these spurs with a narrow connection with the table land, and a wider expanse of surface on the part projecting into the valley. In such cases the works consist of one, two, or three ditches and embankments across the neck, plainly intended to protect the spur against aggression from the table land. The enclosed surface often shows evidence of having been leveled off, the material removed so deposited as to increase the angle of the slope rising from the valley; and in some cases the location of an old footpath leading from the summit into the valley can be clearly traced. The enclosed surface is generally filled with pitholes and shows evidence of long occupancy. The valley of the Cuyahoga is lined with such works, which have been figured and described by Col. Whittlesey. Typical forms of these works are to be seen at the junction of Furnace Run with the Cuyahoga, in Summit County, and at the junction of Payne's Creek with Grand River, in Lake County. These protecting walls and ditches take different shapes, determined by the form of the surface to be protected. Two in Northampton township form complete enclosures with the exception of a single gateway in each opening toward the alluvial bottom land to which doubtless a foot-path originally led. Were these purely military works, or such defences as pertained to the ordinary life of their builders?

These old agriculturists had three enemies against whom they were compelled to contend: the extension of the forests, the intrusions of wild beasts, and the aggressions of more war-like hunting tribes. The extension of the forests is mentioned because it may have been one of the most efficient causes in the final expulsion of these people. Many attempts have been made to find causes for the existence of the treeless prairies of the West. A more natural inquiry would be, how came the other sections to be covered with forests? An herbacious vegetation doubtless preceded the forests and has been slowly restricted by the growth of the latter. In the Southern States extensive regions which sustained only an herbacious vegetation when first explored by the whites, are now covered with trees. Early agriculture attained its highest perfection in regions too arid for forest growth, where facilities were afforded for the artificial irrigation of the cultivated land, and was practically restricted to treeless regions until better cutting tools than our mound builders possessed enabled the argriculturists to successfully contend with forest growth.

These alluvial plains, not long ago covered with water, would be the last to be encroached upon by the forest, and were very probably treeless when first subjected to tillage. Land could not be cleared of forests, and its intrusion could with difficulty be resisted with such tools as have been described above. Crowded out by any causes from these regions, they could not transfer their agricultural operations to the treeless plains of the West, where the rank growth of grass would present so formidable obstacles and where countless herds of buffalo roamed. Certainly they sought these alluvial valleys, poorly adapted to the growth of grass, admirably adapted to the growth of Indian corn; the fortified adjacent bluffs, so selected as to command a view of their cultivated fields below, from whence they could observe the intrusion of man or beast and make provision against the attacks of enemies from the table lands. The size of these enclosures seems to be related to the size of the arable land in the adjacent valley, and hence to the size of the village communities that could be supported from them. It seems a reasonable inference that these enclosures were strongholds, for protection and observation, and designed to meet the normal wants of small communities of argriculturists, and that they were not erected to meet the exigencies of a campaign. The great number of them, and the small size of each, scattered along the bluffs of a single stream, like the Cuyahoga, would tend to confirm this conclusion.

FORT HILL, NEAR BEREA, CUYAHOGA CO.

* A.—Enclosed space; a, a, a,—Embankments and ditches. Scale,200 ft.to the inch.

The wood-cut here introduced indicates the general character of these fortified spurs.

In the valley, and at a distance from these protected enclosures, are sometimes single mounds, which seem not to have been burial mounds raised to such an elevation merely as would give an extended view above the top of the growing corn.

Such an outlying mound may be seen in the Pymatuning Valley, in Wayne, Ashtabula County. In this whole northern region true burial mounds are rare, and those that have been observed are of small size.

In Copley, Summit County, is a fortified enclosure precisely similar to those known to be made by the more modern Indians, and which may probably be referred to them. A large circular elevation rises like an island in the center of a swamp, which, before the adjacent land was cleared, would be almost impassable. This was enclosed by a ditch and and wall, carried entirely around the elevation, making a secret and pretty secure retreat. It is known that the New England Indians secreted in such places their wives and children when at war with the whites, and when discomfited in battle, often retreated to them, sometimes eluding pursuit, sometimes defending themselves there to the last extremity. It is not certain that they enclosed them with embankments of earth.

ISLAND FORT—LOT 14, COPLEY, SUMMIT COUNTY, O., SURVEYED AUGUST 17, 1877.

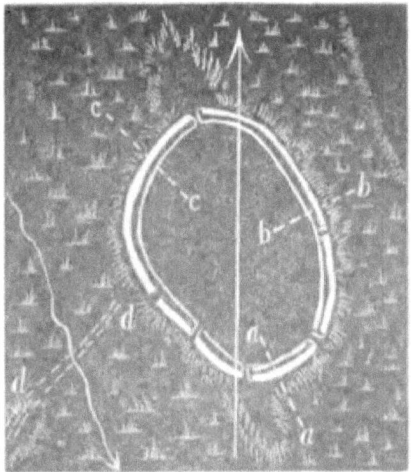

Long diameter, 244 feet; short diameter, 196 feet. Scale, 200 feet to the inch; d, d.—Remains of a beaver dam.

On some of the highest hills of Richland and Knox Counties, are look-out or signal mounds, similar to those which may be traced from these places south to the Ohio River. In some of these places small mounds have been built, with much labor, of stones brought from the valleys below, and nearly all show the results of surface fires. Many of these, and perhaps all of them, may be the work of modern Indians, as it is well known that they were in the habit of telegraphing to scattered members of their tribes or allies by the smoke of fires kindled at such places.

Licking County seems to be the center of population of the old mound builders of the State, and in it are some of the most remarkable earth-works to be found in the United States. Mounds, some of them of large size, some of earth and some of stone, are scattered over the county, but so remarkable are the works near Newark, now in part occupied by the county agricultural society, that comparatively little attention has been given to the others. This collection of mounds, embankments, enclosures, etc., covers over one thousand acres, and by its extent and character indicates that here was the metropolis of the mound builders. The general character of the most important of these works will be better understood by the cut given on another page.

Mr. Smucker has known the works for more than fifty-five years, and hunted over them when covered with the primeval forests. He reports that they were covered with a mixed growth of walnut, sugar-maple, beech, oak, and wild cherry trees, some of which, when cut down, showed that they were over five hundred years old, which would indicate not less than from one thousand to fifteen hundred years since the commencement of the intrusion of the forests. It is believed that General Harrison first called attention to the fact, in regard to similar works, that a mixed forest indicated a forest growth of at least two or three generations of trees. A new natural forest is almost if not quite uniformly composed of one variety only, and the change to a variety of species is made very slowly. But was this ground ever occupied by forests until the abandonment of these works? Their erection with mound builders' tools, if it involved the clearing of a forest as a preliminary work, is so nearly impossible that we can not imagine it would be ever undertaken. It involved not only the clearing of these lands of the forest, but also the neighboring lands which were to be subjected to tillage. It is with the utmost difficulty, in moist and tropical climates, that men armed with the best of steel tools make a successful battle with the forests. It is much more reasonable to suppose that these works were originally located in a treeless region, and the works evidently of the same age scattered over the county indicate that this treeless region was of large extent, covering probably most of the alluvial valley. The inference would follow that the abandonment of the region marked the time when the slow intrusion of the forests reduced the amount of tillable land below the necessities of the community; the time since their abandonment marks the whole period of forest growth on the alluvial bottoms. If the question is asked, how long is this period? the only answer that can be

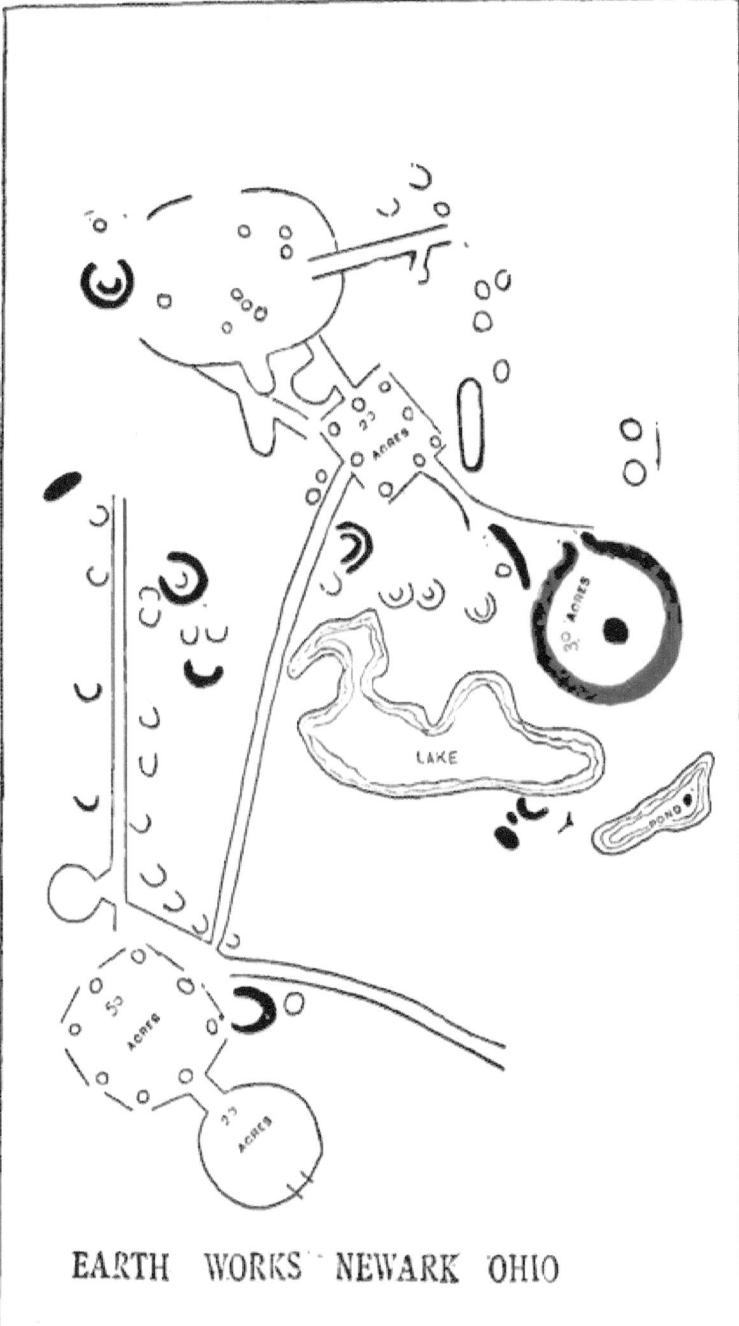

EARTH WORKS NEWARK OHIO

given is that in the term as applied to human history, the time was long; how long, no one can tell.

The most prominent features of these works consist of an octagonal enclosure embracing 50 acres; a square enclosure of 20 acres; a circle of 30 acres, and a smaller circle of 20 acres. A number of covert ways extended from these enclosures, and various mounds, circles and crescentic embankments are connected with them. These walls still rise in places to the height of 30 feet. At the center of the largest circular enclosure is a low mound which Mr. Smucker regards as intended to represent an eagle, with extended wings, measuring from tip to tip of the wings 240 feet, and from head to tail 210 feet. The largest circular enclosure is reported by Mr. Smucker to have an opening about 100 feet wide, and the door-ways in all are much too wide to admit of the idea that any of them are intended for forts. But for what were they designed? A cut of the works at Marietta and of those at Circleville are given for comparison, and to bring out the typical character of this class of earthworks.

The typical characteristics are circular and square, or rectilinear enclosures, the circle with one broad gateway; the square with many gateways, the two either closely connected, as in the Circleville works, or by long covert ways, as in the Newark works. The absence of the circular enclosure, as at Marietta, indicates that it is an adjunct to the other form of enclosure, and may be dispensed with. The presence of something like an altar or symbolic mound in the centre of the circle is also significant. The large number of passage ways into the rectilinear enclosures show that the dominant idea in making these embankments was not to secure a protected enclosure. Yet the protecting of most of these gateways, or breaks in the wall, by mounds, seems to indicate a use of the whole for protecting the interior. The difference in the numbers of the segments of the rectilinear walls should also be noted. In the Circleville enclosure, 8; in the Newark, in one case, 8; in another, 6; in that at Marietta, in

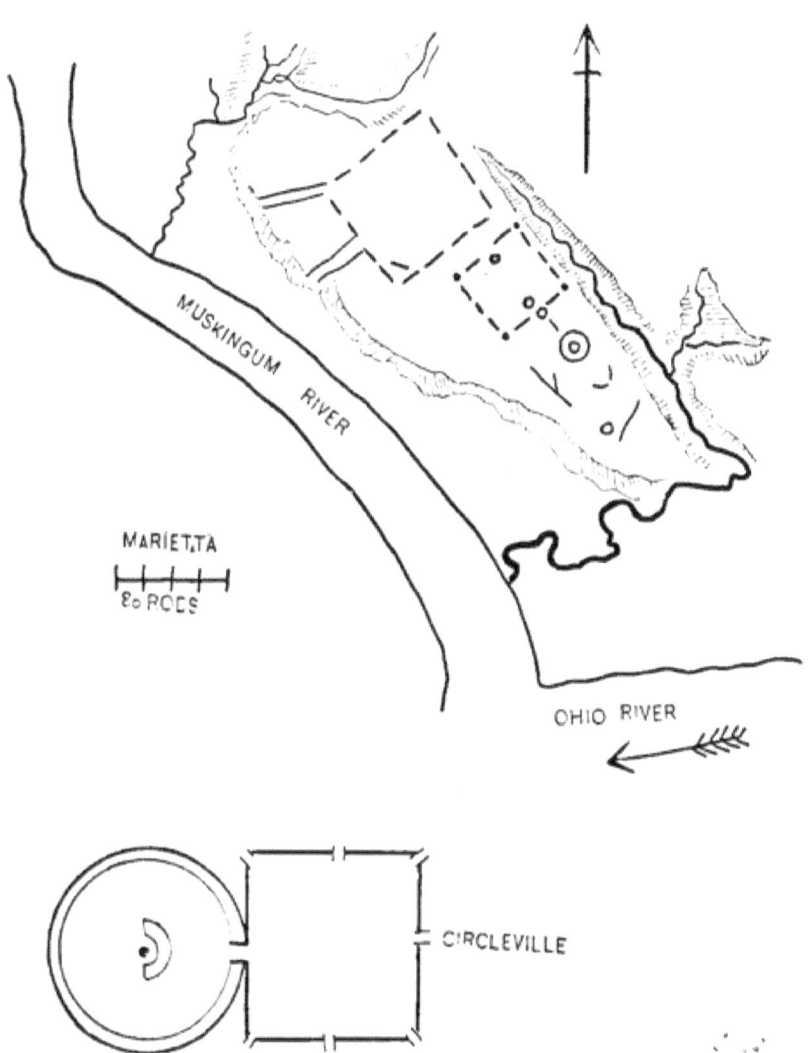

one case,16; in the other,10. Both at Newark and at Marietta there are isolated segments of just such embankments forming no part of an enclosure, but which could be easily imagined to be the beginning of an enclosure.

When Vol. IV. of "Contributions to North American Ethnology," by Lewis H. Morgan, was published, his conclusions, which he advanced, however, as a hypothesis, as simply a possible explanation of the use of these embankments, was not very generally accepted. It must be conceded, however, that he undertook the only line of investigation which could lead to correct conclusions. If we can learn the peculiarities of the social life of the mound builders, we may hope to learn the significance of their remains. The communal life of so many of the American races; the association of so many families in the same dwelling, or connected series of dwellings, which Mr. Morgan shows was characteristic of tribes most nearly allied in other characteristics with the mound builders, makes it a reasonable conclusion that this was a characteristic of their social life, and the theory may well be accepted, as a provisional one, that these segments of embankments of the rectilinear enclosures were the foundations of residences for closely related families of large tribal villages. The enclosures they formed may have contained the store houses of their common supplies, opening also into the circular enclosure which, the central altar-like mound contained in it, suggests was appropriated to religious or ceremonial rites. The single wide opening into these circular enclosures was evidently adapted to the easy ingress and egress of large masses of men. It would follow that they practiced that form of socialism, or communism, which many modern reformers are advocating, which is characteristic of many savage tribes and is always abandoned before any great advance is made in civilization. A clearly defined distinction, universally admitted, between the *tuum* and the *meum* is essential to that personal effort which results in civilization.

The apparent use of the circle for the sacred enclosure confirms the above conclusions, as the circle is the primitive form of building. Our children build circular snow forts, and the birds and beavers build in a circle, because this is the natural form, and most easily made—a form always retained by savages until they learn to build with timber, cut into regular lengths, or with stone. The circle, long used as a sacred enclosure and consecrated by custom, will be retained by a natural conservatism for religious uses long after rectilinear buildings are constructed for common uses.

The engineering skill required for the construction of these works is generally over-estimated. To the eye many of them appear to be perfectly symmetrical. But do we know that they are? They have suffered much from erosion, and it is in every case now impossible to define what was originally the central lines of the embankments or the exact corners of rectilinear enclosures. After all the careful measurements, we do not know the exact dimensions of the base of the great pyramid of Egypt, or whether it is an exact square; the preponderance of evidence being that it is not. No such care has been given to the measurements of any of these enclosures, and it is not proved that any of them are exact geometrical figures. A measuring rod and an instrument for laying down a right angle would suffice for the planing of all of them without a knowledge of any of the principles of geometry.

Associated with these enclosures are many forms of mounds which are also found isolated in various parts of the State, and very abundantly in Licking County. Those that are truncated at the top are usually regarded as temple mounds, and are comparatively rare in Ohio. Explorations in other States show that some of them are true burial mounds. The most noted mound of this character in the United States is located on the rich alluvial land bordering the lower Mississippi, and near the mouth of Cahokia Creek, from which it takes its name. It is ninety feet high, with a base seven hundred feet long, and five hundred feet wide, the level surface at the top measuring four hundred and fifty by two hundred feet, and its solid contents estimated at twenty millions of cubic feet.

Burial mounds are very abundant in this State, of a conical form, generally with a circular, but sometimes with an oval base, usually built of earth, but sometimes of stone. No better idea of the general character of these mounds can be given than is afforded by the following extracts from a paper read before the Connecticut Academy of Arts and Sciences, February 21, 1866, by that careful observer, O. C. Marsh, F. G. S. He says:

" The mound selected for examination was about two and a half miles south of Newark, on the farm of Mr. Thomas Taylor, and was known in the neighborhood as the ' Taylor Mound.' It was conical in form, about ten feet in height, and eighty in diameter at the base, these being about the average dimensions of the burial mounds in that vicinity. It was situated on the summit of a ridge, in the midst of a stately forest. * * * The mound stood quite alone, nearly half a mile from its nearest neighbor, and about three miles from the large earthworks already mentioned. * * *

" An excavation about eight feet in diameter was first made from the apex of the mound, and after the surface soil was removed, the earth was found to be remarkably compact, probably owing to its having been firmly trodden down when deposited. This earth was a light loam, quite different from the soil of the ridge itself, and its peculiar mottled appearance indicated that it had been brought to the spot, in small quantities. In excavating the first five feet, which was a slow and very laborious undertaking, nothing worthy of notice was observed except some traces of ashes, and pieces of charcoal and flint, scattered about at various depths. At five and a half feet below the surface, where the earth became less difficult to remove, a broken stone pipe was found which had evidently been long in use. It was made of a very soft limestone, containing fragments of small fossil shells, apparently cretaceous species. No rock of precisely this kind is known to exist in Ohio. Pieces of a tube of the same material, and about an inch in diameter, were found near the pipe. The cavity was about two-thirds of an inch in diameter, and had been bored with great regularity. Similar tubes have occasionally been found in mounds, but their use is not definitely known.

"About seven feet from the top of the mound a thin white layer was observed, which extended over a horizontal surface of several square yards. Near the centre of this space, and directly under the apex of the mound, a string of more than one hundred beads of native copper was found, and with it a few small bones of a child about three years of age. The beads were strung on a twisted cord of coarse vegetable fibre, apparently the inner bark of a tree, and this had been preserved by the salts of the copper, the antiseptic properties of which are well known. The position of the beads showed clearly that they had been wound two or three times around the neck of the child; and the bones themselves (the neural arches of the cervical vertebrae, a clavicle and a first rib) were precisely those which the beads would naturally come in contact with when decomposition of the body ensued. The remains evidently owe their preservation to this fact, as they are all colored with carbonate of copper, and the other parts of the skeleton have entirely decayed. The position the body had occupied, however, was still clearly indicated by the darker color of the earth. The beads were about one-fourth of an inch long and one-third in diameter, and no little skill had been displayed in their construction. They were evidently made without the aid of fire, by hammering the metal in its original state; but the joints were so neatly fitted that in most cases it was very difficult to detect them. On the same cord, and arranged at regular intervals, were five shell beads of the same diameter, but about twice as long as those of copper. All had apparently been well polished, and the necklace when worn must have formed a tasteful and striking ornament.

"About a foot below the remains just described, and a little east of the centre of the mound, were two adult human skeletons, lying one above the other, and remarkably well preserved. The interment had evidently been performed with great care. The heads were toward the east, slightly higher than the feet, and the arms were carefully composed at the sides. A white stratum, similar in every respect to the one already mentioned, was here very distinct, and extended horizontally over a space of five or six yards, in the centre of which the remains had been laid. The earth separated readily through this stratum, and an examination of the exposed surfaces showed that they were formed from two decayed layers of bark, on one of which the body had been placed, and the other covered over them. The smooth sides of the bark had thus come together and the decomposition of the inner layers had produced the peculiar white substance, as a subsequent microscopic examination clearly indicated. (This white layer, which was thought by Squire and Davis to be the remains of matting, is a characteristic feature in burial mounds. It has only been found where the interments were unquestionably of mound builders.) Directly above these skeletons was a layer of reddish earth, apparently a mixture of ashes and burned clay, which covered a surface of about a square yard. Near the middle of this space was a small pile of charred human bones, the remains of a skeleton, which had been burned immediately over those just described. The fire had evidently been continued for some time, and then allowed to go out; when the fragments of bone and cinders that remained were scraped together, and covered with earth. All the bones were in small pieces, and most of them distorted by heat; but among them were found the lower extremity of a humerus and some fragments of a fibula, which showed them to be human, and indicated an adult rather below the medium size. The two skeletons found beneath these remains were well formed and of opposite sex. The ossification of the bones indicated that the female was about thirty years of age, and the male somewhat older.

"It is not impossible that these were husband and wife, the latter put to death and buried above the remains of her consort; and the charred bones may have been those of a human sacrifice slain at the funeral ceremonies. Near these skeletons was a small quantity of reddish brown powder, which proved on examination to be hematite. It was probably used as a paint.

"On continuing our excavations about a foot lower, and somewhat more to the eastward, a second pile of charred human bones was found, resting on a layer of ashes, charcoal and burned clay. But one or two fragments of these remains could be identified as human, and these also indicated a small-sized adult. The incremation had apparently been performed in the same manner as in the previous instance. Immediately beneath the clay deposit, a third white layer was observed, quite similar to that just described. In this layer was a male skeleton, not in as good preservation as those already mentioned, although belonging to an individual considerably older. In this case, also, the head was toward the east, and the burial had been carefully performed. Near this skeleton about a pint of white chaff was found which appeared to belong to some of the native grasses. The form was still quite distinct, although nearly all the organic substance had disappeared. A few inches deeper, near the surface of the natural earth, several skeletons, of various ages, were met with, which had evidently been buried in a hurried manner. All were nearly or quite horizontal, but no layer of bark had been spread for their reception, and no care taken in regard to the arrangement of limbs. These skeletons were in a tolerable state of preservation, some parts being quite perfect. A tibia and fibula, with most of the corresponding bones of a foot, were found quite by themselves, and well preserved.

"Our excavations had now reached the original surface of the ridge, on which the mound was erected, and we were about to discontinue further researches, when the dark color of the earth at one point attracted attention, and an examination soon showed that a cist or grave had first been excavated in the soil before the mound itself was commenced. This grave was under the eastern part of the elevation, about four feet from the center. It consisted of a simple excavation in an east and west direction, about six feet long, three wide, and nearly two deep. In this grave were found parts of at least eight skeletons, which had evidently been thrown in carelessly—most of them soon after death, but one or two not until the bones had become detached and weathered. Some of the bones were very well preserved, and indicated individuals of various ages. Two infants, about a year and eighteen months old respectively, were each represented by a single os illium, and bones of several other small children were found. One skull, apparently that of a boy, about twelve years of age, was recovered in fragments, and this was the best preserved of any obtained in the mound. The skeleton of an aged woman of small stature was found resting on its side. It was bent together and lay across the grave, with its head toward the north. Some of the loose human bones, exhumed from the bottom of the grave, were evidently imperfect when thrown in. Among these was part of a large femur, which had been gnawed by some carniverous animal. The marks of the teeth were sharply defined, and corresponded to those made by a dog or wolf.

"Quite a number of implements of various kinds were found with the human remains in this grave. Near its eastern end, where the detached bones had been buried, were nine lance and arrow-heads, nearly all of the same form, and somewhat rudely made of flint and chert. * * * These weapons are of peculiar interest, as it appears they are the first that have been discovered in a sepulchral mound, although many such have been carefully examined. They show that the custom—so common among the Indians of this country—of burying with the dead their implements of war or the chase, obtained occasionally, at least, among the mound builders. Not far from these weapons six small hand-axes were found, one of which was made of hematite, and the rest of compact greenstone or diorite, the material often used by the Indians for similar articles. Two of these corresponded closely in form with the stone hand-axe figured by Squire and Davis, as the only one then known from the mounds. With these axes were found a small hatchet of hematite, a flint chisel, and a peculiar flint instrument, apparently used for scraping wood.

"In the central part of the grave, near the aged female skeleton already alluded to, were a large number of bone implements, all exceedingly well preserved. Among these were five needles or bodkins, from three to six inches in length, neatly made from the metatarsal bones of the common deer, and also a spatula cut from an ulna and probably used for moulding pottery. With these were found about a dozen peculiar implements formed from the antlers of a deer and elk. They are cylindrical in form, from three to eight inches in length, and an inch to an inch and a half in diameter. Most of these had both ends somewhat rounded, and perfectly smooth, as if they had either been long in use, or carefully polished. It is possible these instruments were used for smoothing down the seams of skins or leather; they would at least be well adapted to such a purpose. A whistle made from a tooth of a young black bear, and several 'spoons,' cut out of the shells of river mussels, were also obtained from near the same spot.

"A vessel of coarse pottery was found near the western end of the grave, but unfortunately was broken in removing it. It was about five inches in its greatest diameter, six in height, and one-third of an inch in thickness. It was without ornament, and rudely made of clay containing some sand and powdered quartz. It was filled with soft, black earth, the color being probably due to some animal or vegetable substance, which it contained when deposited in the grave. Fragments of a vase of similar material, but having the top ornamented, were found in another part of the mound. Neither of these vessels were superior in any respect to the pottery manufactured by the Indians.

"Near the bottom of the mound, and especially in the grave, were various animal bones, most of them in an excellent state of preservation. Many of them belonged to the common deer, and nearly all the hollow bones had been skillfully split open lengthwise—probably for the purpose of extracting the marrow—a common custom among rude nations. * * *

"The skeletons found in this mound were of medium size, somewhat smaller than the average of the Indians still living in this country. The bones were certainly not stouter than those of Indians of the same size, although this has been regarded as a characteristic of the remains of the mound builders. All the skulls in the mound were broken—in one instance, apparently before burial—and most of them so much decayed that no attempt was made to preserve them. Two, however, were recovered with the more important parts but little injured. Both were of small size, and showed the vertical occiput, prominent vertex and large interparietal diameter so characteristic of crania belonging to the American race. In other respects there was nothing of special interest in their conformation. With a single exception all the human teeth observed were perfectly sound. The teeth of all the adult specimens were much worn, those of aged individuals usually to a remarkable degree. The manner in which these were worn away is peculiarly interesting, as it indicates that the mound builders, like the ancient Egyptians, and the Danes of the stone age, did not, in eating, use their incisive teeth for cutting as modern nations do. This is evident from the fact that the worn incisors are all truncated in the same plane with the coronal surfaces of the molars, showing that the upper front teeth infringe directly on the summits of those below, instead of lapping over them. This peculiarity may be seen in the teeth of Egyptian mummies, as was first pointed out by Cuvier. * * *

"One of the most remarkable features in the mound was the large number of skeletons it contained. With one or two exceptions none of the burial mounds, hitherto examined, have contained more than a single skeleton which unquestionably belonged to the mound builders, while in this instance parts of at least seventeen were exhumed. The number of small children represented among these remains is also worthy of notice, as it indicates, for this particular case, a rate of infant mortality (about thirty-three per cent.) which is much higher than some have supposed ever existed among such nations. Another point of special interest in this mound is the evidence it affords that the regular method of burial among the mound builders was sometimes omitted, and the remains interred in a hurried and careless manner. This was the case with eleven of the skeletons exhumed in the course of our explorations, a remarkable fact, which appears to be without a precedent in the experience of previous investigators. It should be mentioned in this connection that nearly all these remains were those of women and children. Their hurried and careless burial might seem to indicate a want of respect on the part of their surviving friends, were there not ample evidence to prove that reverence for the dead was a prominent characteristic of the mound builders. It is not unlikely that in this instance some unusual cause, such as pestilence, or war, may have made a hasty interment necessary. The various implements and remains of animals found with these skeletons also deserve notice, as they far exceed in number and variety any hitherto discovered in a single mound. They prove, moreover, that if in this instance the rites of regular burial were denied the deposited, their supposed future wants were amply provided for. The contents of one part of the cist, (which is itself a very unusual accompaniment of a mound) appears to indicate that the remains of those who died at a distance from home, were collected for burial, sometimes long after death. The interesting discovery of weapons, which were found with these detached bones, would seem to imply, that in this case the remains and weapons of a hunter or warrior of distinction, recovered after long exposure, had been buried together.

"The last three interments in this mound were performed with great care, as already stated, and in strict accordance with the usual custom of the mound builders. The only point of particular interest in regard to them is the connection which appears to exist between some of the skeletons and the charred human bones found above them. Similar deposits of partially burned bones, supposed to be human, have in one or two instances been observed on the altars of sacrificial mounds, and occasionally in mounds devoted to sepulture, but their connection with the human remains buried in the latter, if indeed any existed, appears to have been overlooked. Our explorations, which were very carefully and systematically conducted, clearly demonstrated that in these instances the incremation had taken place directly over the tomb, and evidently before the regular interment was completed; taking these facts in connection with what the researches of other investigators have made known concerning the superstitious rites of this mysterious people, it seems natural to conclude that in each of these cases a human victim was sacrificed as a part of the funeral ceremonies, doubtless as a special tribute of respect to a person of distinction."

These copious extracts from the report of Mr. Marsh, of his explorations of a mound, doubtless erected by the constructors of the Newark works, is given, for the important information it affords as to the character of these people, and because the minute and pains-taking care exhibited by him in the exploration may well be taken as a model to guide others in similar explorations.

If all the mounds in Ohio, not less than ten thousand in number, were as carefully explored, it would throw a flood of light upon the character and social condition of their builders.

Mounds of observation are usually smaller than the last, generally occupying elevated places constituting a series of signal stations, and sometimes located on alluvial plains in positions commanding an extensive view up and down the valley. Natural elevations often show, by the accumulation of charcoal and burned stones, that they were used as signal stations; but whether these were used by the mound builders or by the more modern Indians, can not be determined, but it is probable they were used by both for this purpose, as were also the burial mounds when properly located.

A large number of still smaller mounds are called, and probably correctly, altar mounds. They are usually connected with other works and include altar-like constructions of stone or clay on which are found ashes, charcoal, calcined bones, some of which have been identified as human, and specimens of nearly all the domestic and military utensils and ornaments of the mound builders. The circular enclosures, as in the instances above given, often have such mounds at the center.

Of effigy mounds there are comparatively few in the State, but among these the Serpent Mound, of Adams County, and the so-called Alligator Mound, of Licking County, are conspicuous examples. They are so well known, and have been so often described, that a repetition of the descriptions here is unnecessary. The so-called Alligator Mound is a very poor imitation of an alligator, having a long tail curved in a manner that no American animal could imitate, except the opossum. The walls of Fort Ancient, in Warren County, have been described as two huge serpents, but the early plats of it show nothing to justify this description.

MINING BY THE MOUND BUILDERS.

The extensive pre-historic copper mines of Lake Superior, first accurately described by Col. Whittlesey, are without doubt the work of the mound builders, and the source from which they obtained the greater part of the material for their copper implements and ornaments. Some of it they doubtless obtained from the drift. These mines were opened by means of their rude tools, with great labor, wooden shovels being used in removing waste material. The rock enclosing the copper was subjected to the action of fire, and broken up by stone hammers and mauls. Pieces from the masses too large to handle were laboriously cut or pounded off with their stone axes, and pieces too large to be handled in any other manner were slowly raised to the surface by prying up the alternate sides, placing small timbers beneath and building them up under the load in the form of a log house. The copper thus obtained was sometimes worked into implements in the neighborhood of the mines, as important finds in that region show. Several copper spears and knives have been found together, showing that they were not accidently lost but buried for safe keeping. The great abundance of mica found in the mounds is evidence that the builders made long journeys to engage in mica mining, or maintained a system of exchanges with those who worked the mines. This mineral was held in high esteem, and was obtained in large quantities. Skeletons have been exhumed entirely covered with it.

Masses of galena have been found in Ohio mounds too large to have been obtained in the State, and which were doubtless the product of galena mining. Lead is so easily obtained from galena that it would be strange if the mound builders did not stumble upon the mode of reducing this ore, but the metal would not be of great value to them. In the State Collection is a lead ornament found in the ditch within the great Circleville enclosure; but the form is so much like that of the lead tomahawks the school-boys made, when they used lead to rule their writing paper, that it is reasonably inferred that it is of modern manufacture.

Salt was evidently manufactured from natural brine springs by some of the native races in other localities, but the evidence is wanting of its manufacture within the present limits of this State.

In the "oil territory" of Trumbull County, are prehistoric wells which were apparently sunk to obtain petroleum, but whether the work of mound builders or of the more recent tribes, is not apparent. It is known that the Indians highly prized the petroleum from springs, and used it as a medicine.

ALPHABETIC WRITING AND ENGRAVED TABLETS.

On the present site of Cincinnati, at its first discovery by the whites, was a series of mounds, earth-works and embankments, which, according to the account given by General Harrison, were among the most extensive in the State. In one of these mounds, explored in 1841, was found, as it is alleged, the "Cincinnati tablet," which has given rise to much discussion, and has been classed among the "frauds" by expert and conscientious archaeologists; but the vindication of its authenticity, published by Mr. Robert Clark, of Cincinnati, in 1876, may be regarded as fully satisfactory and as entitling it to a place among the authentic relics of the mound builders. It is made of a dark, fine-grained sandstone, and as no verbal description could be made to convey an intelligible idea of it, a cut of both sides of it, of full size, is here given, which was kindly loaned for this use by Mr. Clark. An inspection of the cuts will lead to the ready inference that it is not a writing of any kind. There are slight differences between the engraving and a cast of the relic. In the cast the two bars at one end of the tablet are each connected at the middle with the central work, so that all that is included within the outer margins constitutes one

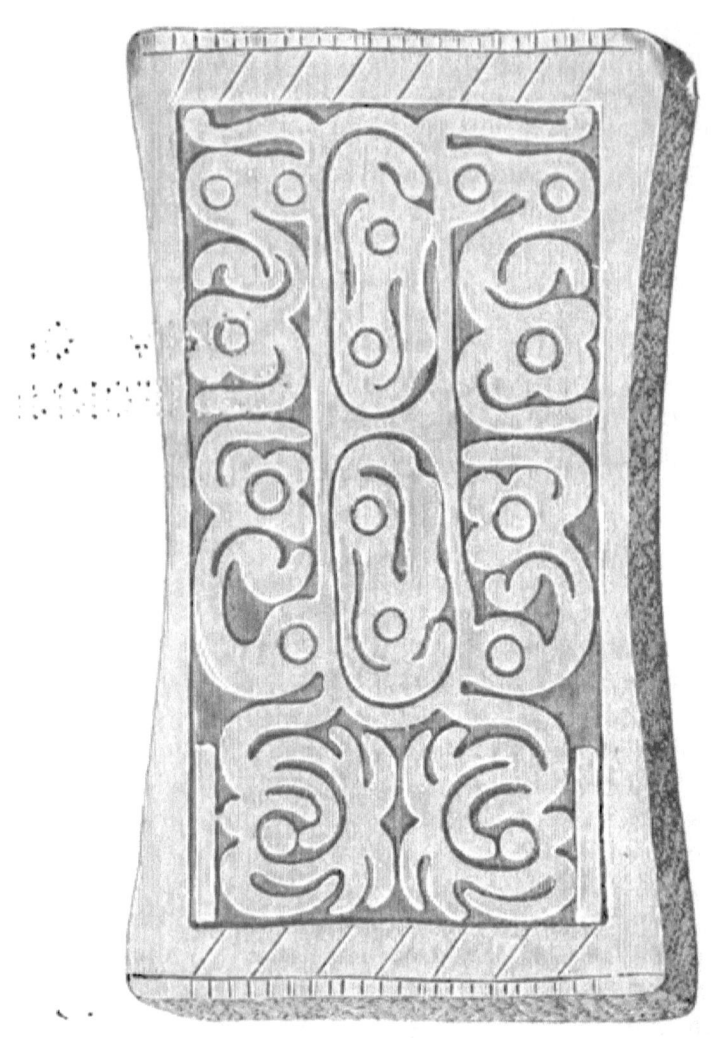

CINCINNATI TABLET.

CINCINNATI TABLET, REVERSE.

figure with bilateral symmetry. It is a work showing much skill in stone-engraving, both in the execution and in the almost exact duplication of the separate parts, but its signification, if it has any, is not apparent. The supposition that the conspicuous markings at the two ends are copies of standard measures of length is scarcely tenable, when it is noted that in the cast neither of the series of divisions are of equal length and that the smaller are not subdivisions of the larger. Mr. Clark sends me a photograph of a somewhat similar engraving said to have been found in a mound. It is smaller, very much less skillfully executed, and lacks the bilateral symmetry of the "Cincinnati tablet." A cut of the reverse side of the latter is given, but it probably has no significance.

The sand-stone tablet, alleged to have been found at Wilmington, is in some respects like the "Cincinnati tablet." According to the engravings published it is far inferior in execution. There is only a partial attempt at bilateral symmetry, and the duplication of parts is inaccurately done. This, and the unintelligible carving on the slate ornament, might pass as genuine relics were it not for the character of the animal and human carvings on the other part of it. The free-hand attempt at shading the animal figures, the graceful outlines of the human figures, the delineation of their clothing, particularly the close-fitting garments of the male, and the character of the weapons he carries, which have been previously described, all indicate that they do not represent barbaric art. A doubt of their genuineness is no imputation upon the integrity of those who have given descriptions of them to the public. The best collections of relics contain forgeries, some of which have been purchased for a large price, and almost every community can furnish those who will take great delight in imposing upon explorers of mounds. If the genuineness of all these relics were conceded, they do not afford, as is claimed, any evidence of the use of writing. What are claimed to be written characters in all of the squares, are laboriously unlike in all their details. A writing of that length, either alphabetical, pictorial or symbolical, would certainly exhibit repetitions.

The controversy over the Hebrew inscriptions, claimed to have been found by David Wyrick, near Newark, is now generally regarded as closed. They were found when evidence was eagerly sought to connect the aboriginal races with the house of Israel. Now that the idea of such a connection is abandoned by all, the discovery of Hebrew inscribed stones would be an anachronism, for such forgeries will always in some way represent the ideas of the time of the forgery. As an example, the greatest forgery of this century is the book of Mormon. A careful reading of it will disclose to any competent critic very nearly the date of the forgery. It was written during, or very soon after, the controversy between Masonry and Anti-Masonry, and is decidedly Anti-Masonic. It was written during the theological controversy over popery pedo-baptism; the salvation of infants; a paid priesthood, election and free-will, all of which questions it attempts to settle; when the "falling power," as it was called, was regarded as the work of the Spirit, which it describes and approves; while the act of divination by looking into a crystal was believed in by some; while it was believed that the native races here were Israelites; and before contact with Europeans, worshipers of the Great Spirit, and while it was popularly believed that the linguistic peculiarities of our bible were wholly characteristic of the languages in which it was originally written, and not of the state of the English language at the time of its translation. These internal evidences fix the date of its composition as about fifty years ago.

Mr. Wyrick's first find was the inscribed key-stone in the form of a Masonic emblem on which was carved in Hebrew of the twelfth century. "The King of the Earth." "The Word of the Lord." "The Laws of Jehovah." "The Holy of Holies." In the year following he "found," enclosed in a neat stone box with a closely fitting cover, a stone tablet having on it an effigy of Moses in priestly robes and an epitome of the ten commandments in Hebrew. Surely no better evidence could be secured of a Hebrew migration to this country. It is significant that Mr. Wyrick's published account of the "finds" was largely devoted to an attempt to prove that they could not be forged, and that upon his death there was found in his working-room a Hebrew Bible which doubtless aided him much in finding Hebrew inscriptions.

These Holy relics were sold to David M. Johnson, of Coshocton, Ohio, who in 1867 employed laborers for several days in exploring a mound from which one of the inscribed stones, he obtained from Wyrick, was taken. His search was rewarded by finding *inside of a human skull* a conical stone about three (3) inches long on which was also a Hebrew inscription. No one seems to have been surprised by the peculiarity of the place in which it was found, or to have doubted its genuineness. It is probable that no archaeologist of fair standing can now be found to advocate its genuineness or that of the Wyrick finds.

Perhaps no relic has been the cause of more discussion in Ohio, and among archaeologists everywhere, than a small piece of sand-stone covered on one face with inscribed characters and which it is alleged was taken from a vault in the Grave Creek Mound, in 1838. Some years ago, as one of a committee appointed for that purpose by the Ohio State Archaeological Society, I undertook to gather up all the evidence that could be secured in regard to the finding of this relic. Numerous letters were received from those engaged in the exploration, or who were present when it was found. All answered every inquiry fully and frankly. These letters were turned over to the Northern Ohio Historical Society, of Cleveland, for preservation. From all these letters it may be regarded as well established—

First. That this relic was first seen in the loose dirt, wheeled out through a tunnel leading to the centre of the mound, and dumped in a pile, from which it was picked up and exhibited to those standing by, all at once assuming that it came from the mound.

Second. That no one questioned its genuineness or gave it any scrutiny to see whether it showed evidence of recent manufacture. Hence the character of the inscription can now be determined only by an examination of it, or of engravings of it.

It is very easy to manufacture a series of arbitrary characters which would constitute a good alphabet. It is not so easy to forge an inscription with it. In an inscription the letters will be duplicated, or doubled, and will be repeated with a frequency in an inverse ratio to the number of the characters in the alphabet used. The forger of an inscription will proceed very much as if forging an alphabet, and it will rarely occur to him to double or repeat his characters. In a forged alphabet, also, a genetic relation will frequently be observed between letters and those immediately preceding, the one being a modification of the other. In using the same letters in an intelligible inscription this connection will be broken.

To illustrate these facts, four different persons were asked to write each an inscription in arbitrary characters, unlike the letters of any alphabet they knew, and without being informed as to the object of the request. These inscriptions are here copied, and all of the characters except the last two of the Grave Creek Mound inscription:

No. 1. By a teacher and law student.
" 2. By a school girl.
" 3. By a druggist.
" 4. By a college professor.
" 5. The Graw Creek inscription.

The latter may be compared with an engraving copied from the stone, which is here inserted:

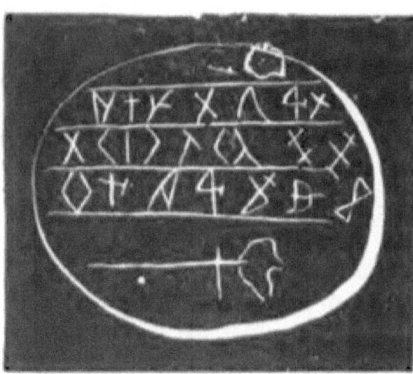

The genetic relations between different successive characters can be clearly seen in all these inscriptions, that from the Grave Creek Mound, included. The writer of each often had one character in mind when making the next one, and gave a modified form of it.

There is no doubling of letters in any of them, and there is no certain repetition of letters. In the Grave Creek inscription, the 4th from the left, is somewhat like the 8th, and the 6th somewhat like the 20th. In a cast of the stone these characters are more unlike than in the engraving. If it is conceded that there are two repetitions, it will be found that taking a sentence of equal length from any known alphabetical writing, the repetitions will be much more numerous. The inference is that the inscription is not alphabetical, an inference greatly strengthened by the smallness of the characters, the fineness and distinctness of the lines forming them. The character of the tools for writing on stone, which the mound builders must have used, if they wrote at all, is apparent from the preceding pages. This inscription requires for its production as good an instrument as a sharp-pointed steel knife. With that it could easily be produced in a very few minutes.

As the case now stands, it can well be said that there is no evidence that the mound builders knew or practiced the art of writing. Further, that their social and artistic condition, as disclosed by the study of their remains, was not such as to make the discovery of the art of writing probable.

SOCIAL AND CIVIL CONDITION OF THE MOUND BUILDERS.

The social condition of the American hunting Indians has been pretty thoroughly known through the direct contact of the civilized nations; but that of the "mound builders" is not so easily learned. A special definition of this term is a necessary preliminary to the investigation, for many of the hunting races, inhabiting the country after the advent of the whites, were mound builders, and the erection of mounds, especially in the southern part of the territory now including the United States, was continued to quite modern times. Articles of copper, silver and steel, of unquestioned modern manufacture, are found in southern mounds as deeply and securely buried as the implements found in Ohio mounds. The term, unless the context otherwise shows, will be used to designate the builders of the elaborate structures found in Ohio annd the other works attributed to the same age.

The facts above recorded, as well as the concurrent testimony of all the well established facts, show the want of three very important aids to civilization: domestic animals, iron or steel tools, and the art of writing. The want of the first is almost an inseparable obstacle to emergence from barbarism. The pastoral condition which was here impossible, is normally the first advance from the hunting condition. Flocks and herds are the first important accumulations of capital for distant future use, and their possession leads man out of the savage habit of content if his immediate wants are supplied, and induces labor and forethought for the future. The flesh, skin, milk and wool of these animals provides more abundantly for his wants, developes arts for preparing and utilizing them, secures a more compact social organization, and less vagrant habits. These lead upward to the practice of the art of agriculture and a special appropriation of land interfering with its pastoral use, followed by controversies like that between Cain and Abel, in which the agriculturist is generally victorious, because his is the superior condition, leading to further advancement. It is not without significance that the descendants of Cain were represented as the discoverers of the arts of metallurgy. The single domestic animal of the Peruvians, valuable for food, as a beast of burden, and for its wool, gave them a great advantage over all other American tribes. Its wool developed the art of spinning and weaving, gave them better clothing, and with many other important advantages, gave them the use of sails and the art of navigation. North America, with its deeply indented coast line, was more favorable to navigation, but a sailboat was nowhere found by its first European explorers.

The mound builders reached the agricultural without passing through the pastoral condition, but the want of efficient metal tools must have made that agriculture comparatively unproductive. Their agriculture consolidated them into village communities, gave them a compact, social organization which made the construction of the remarkable works they have left us, possible. If they had stumbled apon the art of producing iron and steel, they would doubtless have attained to a true civilization. Without it we should naturally deem this impossible; and we in fact find that all the relics of the arts they have left us are barbaric. Their sculptures and carvings often show much skill and very patient, long-continued work, but to the modern eye are not artistic. Their clothing must have been of a primitive character. The fragments of textile fabrics preserved are coarse, and the use of strings of bark fibre for their most costly necklaces, as disclosed by remains found in a mound by Mr. Marsh, sufficiently attest the want or scarcity of better spinning fiber. They were doubtless largely clothed in the skins of wild beasts, and they perhaps utilized the wooly hair of the buffalo by spinning and weaving it. They found leisure for the attendance of large concourses at religious or civic festivals, as the elaborate and costly enclosures evidently designed for some such use, abundantly testify. They manufactured pottery, but it was all rude. They made long journeys in search of copper and mined it in the most primitive manner, but they did not learn the art of making castings of it, or of consolidating the small fragments by melting them. They probably sunk wells for petroleum where it could be obtained from seepings through the earth, but no vessel which is suspected to be a lamp for burning it, or animal fats, for light has been discovered. They wrought chert and stone and shells into about as many useful forms as modern workmen could, with their more perfect tools, but these were all very poor substitutes for modern steel tools. They believed in a future life, and provided the dead with the weapons of war and of the chase and the domestic utensils they had used in life and dispatched with them on their long journey their wives and attendants as companions. Their later history was probably that of a long-continued struggle against the aggressions of hostile hunting tribes and the encroachments of forests, before the combined influence of which they were forced to retreat.

Standing beside some of their remarkable earthworks, a glamour of admiration leads us to picture, in imagination, a departed race, learned in all the highest arts of civilization. But under the careful study of their remains the picture vanishes, and leaves in its place that of a patient, plodding people, with poor appliances, struggling towards civilization while still on the confines of barbarism. If we compare the artistic remains found in the mounds with those exhumed on the sites of the most ancient Asiatic cities, the contrast, both in the variety of articles and skill displayed in their production, is very great, and precisely such a contrast as we ought to expect between peoples having good metal cutting tools and those without them.

If it is asked of what race were these mound builders, it now can only be said they were one of the native American races, closely allied to the hunting Indians, and probably a branch of the same race. There are certain peculiarities of the skulls and jaws of the skeletons, found in the mounds, which are supposed by many to separate them from the other native races.

The description of the skulls found by Mr. Marsh, in a mound at Newark, as given in the quotation from his report, indicates the character of these peculiarities, which also characterize a skull obtained from a mound at Marietta, and two obtained from a mound near Chattanooga, Tenn. The lower jaw is larger and more prognathous than that of the modern Indian, and so articulated that the incisors of each jaw meet squarely when the mouth is shut, not passing each other so as to give a scissor-like cutting action, as do the incisors of modern civilized people. Hence the action of the incisors is a grinding and not a cutting action, and these teeth are worn off on the same plane as the molars, and of necessity, just as fast. In none of the jaws of these skulls were there any unsound teeth, but all were remarkably worn away, all of the incisors equally with the molars. This rapid wearing away of the teeth, which is frequently observed in savage races, and is seen in the early British skulls, is the result of eating hard, unground grain, or of a want of neatness in preparing food, leaving it filled with dirt and sand. Ordinarily the latter is the cause. Either is incompatible with much advance in civilization. This form of the jaw and mode of its articulation, which brings the incisors of the two jaws into direct contact, is not, as supposed, peculiar to the mound builders, but is often seen in skulls which plainly belonged to modern Indians, and occasionally in the white race, when the one having that peculiarity is said to have double teeth all round. This peculiarity is seen in a skull taken from an Indian burial ground near Fairport, Lake County. Comparing this skull with that from the Marietta Mound, the following differences are observed: The lower jaw of that from the mound is more massive and more prognathous. The front teeth are larger and all the teeth are more worn; all are sound, while two in the Indian skull were partly decayed. The forehead is narrower and more retreating, and there is a marked occipital protuberance greatly exceeding that on the Indian skull, above which is a suture, below the lamboid suture, which is wanting in the Indian, and in most modern skulls. The supercilliary ridge is more prominent, the molar bones larger, but more retreating; the chin less prominent, the cavities for the eyes less circular, and a little more oblique; and the nasal cavities smaller in the skull from the mound. All the cranial characteristics of the Indian skull, although it is smaller, are of a higher type than are exhibited by the skull from the Marietta mound.

NOTE.—The Indian skull was pierced, while living, through the occipital bone with some sharp cutting instrument, about an inch and a half wide, which pierced the brain, and was evidently the cause of death.

WERE THE MOUND BUILDERS THE FIRST OCCUPANTS OF THIS REGION?

The fire hearths along the banks of the Ohio River, described by Col. Whittlesey and Mr. Thomas W. Kinney, are doubtless of an earlier date than the mounds, but unless the builders of these were an intrusive people, bringing with them their practice of mound-building, they may have occupied the country for centuries before the building of these structures. On the banks of the Tennessee River, between Mussel Shoals and a point a little above Chattanooga, a rude chronology is preserved that is of especial interest. Along the banks of the river are many little shell heaps containing various relics of a rude art which clearly indicate the artificial character of these mounds. Scattered through them are many minute bivalve shells, clearly indicating that the water formerly covered the mounds, and that they were probably the accumulated refuse from residences built on piles over the water. The extent of these mounds indicate long-continued occupancy, and if, as appears, by the occupants of pile-dwellings, this fact can probably be demonstrated by the careful excavation of the earth under and around the shell mounds.

The first terrace above the river is covered with the bleached fragments of river shells, of such a character as to clearly show that the water of the river covered the terrace when these shells, which are of the same species as those now in the river, were deposited. A little above Chattanooga the soil of the terrace is filled with these shells, and here on this terrace is a large sepulchral mound which was partially explored in 1864. It was built up from the alluvial soil of this terrace, and contained large numbers of shells like those scattered upon the surface, so well preserved as to show that the mound was built shortly after the recession of the water, and before the shells were bleached by atmospheric influence. On the same terrace, and close to the mound, is the site of a manufactory of pottery and of chert implements, the material for the latter being very abundant in the immediate neighborhood. The soil is filled with flakes of the chert, with broken and perfect chert implements, as well as with fragments of pottery and amorphous masses of partially burned clay. It is difficult to take up a shovel full of earth without taking with it some of these relics, but not a trace of them was found in the mound, making it certain that its erection preceded the rude manufactory. The shell heaps pertain to a human occupancy when the water of the river covered the first terrace, the building of the mound to an occupancy immediately after the water had fallen to its present channel, and the manufacturing of pottery and chert implements to a time subsequent to the erection of the mound. If the withdrawal of the water from this terrace is to be attributed, as seems probable, to the wearing away of a narrow rock channel of the river directly below Chattanooga, it will carry back the date of the mound and of the preceding shell heaps to a very remote period. The mound is in all respects a typical mound builder's sepulchral mound.

In explanation of a possible find which may astonish some future explorer, it should be stated that the examination of the mound was made during the war, when the land around it was cultivated by the United States Sanitary Commission as a hospital garden. A tunnel was carried in from the east side to the centre of the mound where a chamber of considerable size was excavated. As the walls stood firm, this chamber was utilized by the gardener as a store-house. When all the guns of the forts about Chattanooga were simultaneously discharged in celebration of Lee's surrender, the concussion caused the top of this chamber to fall in, burrying at the center of the mound a large number of modern gardening tools. The top of the mound was restored to shape, the entrance to the tunnel closed, and the tools left to await a resurrection at the hands of an antiquarian.

The last occupancy of the banks of the Tennessee disclosed above was doubtless by modern Indians; the next by the "mound builders," as distinguished from modern mound building Indians. Whether the earliest was that of an earlier stage in the life of the mound builders can not as satisfactorily be determined. The probability is that of different tribes.

The question as to the origin of the mound builders would be answered if the question of the origin of the other native races was solved. Whether the new world, as it is called, which is in fact the old world, was peopled from the old, or the reverse, can not be determined. Linguistic and other evidences indicate a point in Southern Asia, or in a submerged land south of it, from whence an emigration started which gradually spread over all that continent. This, if true, would make it probable that emigration from the same point extended to this continent. This would lead to the inference that it was peopled by some early branch of the Mongolian race, to which the American races are most nearly allied, by the way of Behrings Strait, and the Auletian Islands, perhaps reinforced in South America, as Haeckel suggests, by way of the Pacific Islands, from Southern Asiatic tribes. If this was the case, this emigration was at a very early date, as nearly all the customs, habits, arts, and even languages of the American races seem to be indigenous.

The practice of scalping, common to the American Indians and the ancient Scythians, is the most apparent evidence of race affinities between the people of the two continents. It is evident also that the more civilized American races practiced some forms of the sabian and plallic worship which characterized the earliest known religious culture of Asia, and that the use of the cross was intimately associated with this worship in both continents. The ceremony of baptism, called a new birth, pertained to both, and there are indications of the practice of other rites and ceremonies substantially the same on both continents. But these points of agreement are few, and if not accidental, point to a time anterior to all written history and to a social condition essentially barbaric.

To the finds, as claimed, of a stone carving buried beneath ten feet of glacial drift, in Stark County, and of the antique chert knife in the drift in Summit County, may be added the claim of a find of a beautifully polished stone axe, at the depth of twenty feet, in Ashland County. If these finds are accepted as authentic, we must assume that these articles were manufactured before the close of the glacial epoch. But the Summit County specimen was found where there was only two or three feet of drift clay over the rock surface below, and various causes may have carried it from the surface to that depth.

It is also not claimed that any one saw either of the other specimens in the clay matrix at the bottom of the well. They both appeared in the material dumped from the buckets used in hoisting material from the wells. The evidence of the finding of pre-glacial implements must be so certain as to exclude any other reasonable hypothesis. Such evidence is not afforded in these cases.

In Europe, rude carvings demonstrate the co-existence of man with some of the extinct animals. Such carvings are generally wanting here. But the bones of the elephant and the mastodon are found near the surface, sometimes in marshes that are alternately wet and dry, in a much better state of preservation than some of the human bones at the bottom of burial mounds where the conditions for their preservation are much more favorable. Placing such bones side by side and bearing in mind the places from which they were exhumed, one can not resist the conclusion that the human remains are quite as old as those of these extinct animals. With these facts apparent, there is no intrinsic improbability of the antiquity of the "elephant pipes" in the Davenport collection. The manner in which they were found does not indicate that they were "planted to deceive." They are of the recognized form of the mound builders' pipe, a form not imitated by modern Indians. The preponderance of evidence is in favor of their genuineness, which, if granted, proves the co-existence of the mound builders with the extinct American pachyderms.

Evidence of a very remote human occupancy, approaching the close of the drift period, is not wanting. Mr. Abbott's many finds of "drift implements" are all found in the modified river drift, and while he makes a pretty strong case that this modification occurred at the close of the drift period, the most conservative archaeologists are awaiting the discovery of undoubted human remains in the unmodified drift. Until such a discovery is made, the existence of man at the time of the glacial epoch on this continent will be regarded as an open question.

Addendum.

After this report was completed, Mr. Rufus Chapman, of Garrettsville, Ohio, brought to me an unique specimen, obtained by him from a neighbor who plowed it up in a field at a place where several "Indian relics" had previously been found. It is made of blue porcelain of the form shown in the figure: $11\frac{3}{10}$ inches long, and in diameter, $1\frac{4}{10}$ inches and 1 inch. It is hollow, as is shown by its weight, and by a small fire-crack in one of the grooves through which the cavity can be explored by a stiff hair. It is smooth, very symmetrical, and could be formed only in a carefully prepared mold in two pieces, and the parts attached to each other while the material was plastic. The adhesion of the two parts is perfect, leaving a slight ridge, but no other indication of the place of junction. On one of the ridges, near the end of the piece, is an imperfection, showing that after it was taken from the mold, this place was repaired by the addition of the plastic material, which did not make the ridge at that place perfect.

Mr. Holmes, of the Bureau of Ethnology of the Smithsonian Institute, after an examination of it, says: "No one here has seen anything like it. It is made of porcelain, a material unknown to the American aborigines. It is therefore not aboriginal, and is probably not ancient. It looks as if it might be an implement intended for use in some of the arts—in the manipulation of fiber, skins, leather, or the like. Some one will probably be found who can tell you all about it."

If designed for such use, the reason is not apparent of the greatly increased labor of making it hollow. A wood cut of the specimen is here given, and information solicited from any who have seen similar articles or have any knowledge of the uses to which they were applied. The cut is a little less than one-half natural size.

www.ingramcontent.com/pod-product-compliance
Lightning Source LLC
Chambersburg PA
CBHW020130170426
43199CB00010B/713